communion

Also by bell hooks

Salvation: Black People and Love
All About Love: New Visions
Remembered Rapture: The Writer at Work
A Woman's Mourning Song
Wounds of Passion: A Writing Life
Reel to Real: Race, Sex, and Class at the Movies
Bone Black: Memories of Girlhood
Killing Rage: Ending Racism
Art on My Mind: Visual Politics
Teaching to Transgress: Education as the Practice of Freedom
Outlaw Culture: Resisting Representations
Sisters of the Yam: Black Women and Self-Recovery
Black Looks: Race and Representation
Breaking Bread: Insurgent Black Intellectual Life
(with Cornel West)
Yearning: Race, Gender, and Cultural Politics
Talking Back: Thinking Feminist, Thinking Black
Feminist Theory: From Margin to Center
Ain't I a Woman: Black Women and Feminism

communion

The Female Search for Love

bell hooks

WILLIAM MORROW

An Imprint of HarperCollins*Publishers*

HarperCollins books may be purchased for educational, business, or sales promotional use. For information please write: Special Markets Department, HarperCollins Publishers Inc., 10 East 53rd Street, New York, NY 10022.

FIRST EDITION

Printed on acid-free paper

Library of Congress Cataloging-in-Publication Data

Hooks, Bell.
    Communion : the female search for love / Bell Hooks.—1st ed.
        p.   cm.
    ISBN 0-06-621442-4 (hc. : alk. paper)
    1. Women—History.   2. Feminism.   3. Women—Social conditions.
    4. Self-perception in women.   5. Man-woman relationships.   I. Title.

HQ1154 .H635   2002
305.4'09—dc21
                                                    2001044711

02   03   04   05   06   RRD   10   9   8   7   6   5   4   3   2   1

To all of you who dance with me in the circle of love—
To Anthony with whom I whirl and whirl and whirl

There is an eros present at every meeting, and this is also sacred. One only has to listen inwardly to the histories and resonances of the word we use for religious experience. In Sanskrit the word *satsang,* which translates into English as "meeting," means "godly gathering." In the English language the word *common* is linked through the word "communicate" to "communion." . . . To exist in a state of communion is to be aware of the nature of existence.

—SUSAN GRIFFIN

Contents

CONTENTS

CONTENTS

the soul seeks communion

Women talk about love. From girlhood on, we learn that conversations about love are a gendered narrative, a female subject. Our obsessions about love begin not with the first crush or the first fall. They begin with that first recognition that females matter less than males, that no matter how good we are, in the eyes of a patriarchal universe we are never quite good enough. Femaleness in patriarchal culture marks us from the very beginning as unworthy or not as worthy, and it should come as no surprise that we learn to worry most as girls, as women, about whether we are worthy of love.

Raised with competitive, fault-finding mothers and fathers whom we can never really please or in a world where we are the "perfect" Daddy's girl who fears losing his approval to the point where we stop eating, stop growing up because we see Daddy losing interest, because we see he does not love women, we are uncertain about love. To keep his love we must cling to girlhood at all costs. All girls continue to be taught when they are young, if not by their parents then by the culture around them, that they must earn the right to be loved—that "femaleness" is not good enough. This is a female's first lesson in the school of patriarchal thinking and values. She must earn love. She is not entitled. She must be good to be loved. And good is always defined by someone else, someone on the outside. Writing about her relationship with her dad in the essay "Dancing on My Father's Shoes," Patricia Ruff offers a heartrending account of losing the sense of being worthy of love, of being valued, confessing, "My mother told me that he wanted a daughter first and couldn't have been more delighted when he got me. So I was unprepared when my princess status, quite without warning, was ripped away raggedly, like a sheet of paper torn from a notebook. Something happened that no one explained to me. . . . I had no voice for my feeling and was without words for the anger and pain over his being suddenly beyond reach." Concerned that her younger sister might feel the same pain of being emotionally rejected, Ruff suggested that they confront their father together: "We burst into their bedroom, threw ourselves on our stunned father, who remained stone still and speechless as we cried all over him, grabbing him, holding on, not wanting to let go. 'Daddy, please hold us, tell us you love us, we love you, we need you to love us,' we begged." Rejection and abandonment by fathers and mothers is the space of lack that usually sets the stage for female desperation to find and know love.

Often girls feel deeply cared about as small children but then find as we develop willpower and independent thought that the world stops affirming us, that we are seen as unlovable. This is the insight Madonna Kolbenschlag shares in *Lost in the Land of Oz* about the nature of a female's fate: "In some fundamental way, we have all been deprived of love, of mothering—if not of love, then of the feeling that we have been loved. Knowing we were loved is not enough; we have to *feel* it." How can any girl sustain the belief that she is loved, truly loved, when all around her she sees that femaleness is despised? Unable to change the fact of femaleness, she strives to make herself over, to become someone worthy of love.

Schooled to believe that we find ourselves in relation with others, females learn early to search for love in a world beyond our own hearts. We learn in childhood that the roots of love lie outside our capabilities, that to know love we must be loved by others. For as females in patriarchal culture, we cannot determine our self-worth. Our value, our worth, and whether or not we can be loved are always determined by someone else. Deprived of the means to generate self-love, we look to others to render us lovable; we long for love and we search.

While contemporary feminist movement critiqued the devaluation of the female that begins in girlhood, it did not change it. Today's girls grow up in a world where they will learn from many quarters that women are the equals of men, but there is still no real place for feminist thinking and practice in girlhood. Girls today struggle against sexist defining roles in the same ways that girls did before the contemporary feminist movement. While strands of feminism here and there support that struggle, more often than not, girls feel besieged by the mixed messages that come from being born into a world where women's liberation has been given a small place even as girls remained trapped in the arms of patriarchy. A measure of that entrapment is the widespread fear among all girls, irrespective of race or class, that they will not be loved.

Within patriarchal culture, the girl who does not feel loved in her family of origin is given another chance to prove her worth when she is encouraged to seek love from males. Schoolgirl crushes, mad obsessions, compulsive longings for male attention and approval indicate that she is rightly pursuing her gendered destiny, on the road to becoming the female who can be nothing without a man. Whether she is heterosexual or homosexual, the extent to which she yearns for patriarchal approval will determine whether she is worthy to be loved. This is the emotional uncertainty that haunts the lives of all females in patriarchal culture.

From the start, then, females are confused about the nature of love. Socialized in the false assumption that we will find love in the place where femaleness is deemed unworthy and consistently devalued, we learn early to pretend that love matters more than anything, when in actuality we know that what matters most, even in the wake of feminist movement, is patriarchal approval. From birth on, most females live in fear that we will be abandoned, that if we step outside the approved circle, we will not be loved.

Given our early obsessions with seducing and pleasing others to affirm our worth, we lose ourselves in the search to be accepted, included, desired. Our talk about love has heretofore primarily been a talk about desire. For the most part, the feminist movement did not change female obsession with love, nor did it offer us new ways to think about love. It told us that we were better off if we stopped thinking about love, if we could live our lives as though love did not matter, because if we did not do so we were in danger of becoming a member of a truly despised female category: "the woman who loves too much." The irony, of course, is that most of us were not loving too much; we were not loving at all. What we were was emotionally needy, desperate for the recognition (whether from male or female partners) that would prove our worth, our value, our right to be alive on the planet, and we were willing to do anything to get it. As females in a patriarchal culture, we were not slaves of love; most of us were and are slaves of longing—yearning for a master who will set us free and claim us because we cannot claim ourselves.

Feminism offered us the promise that a culture would be created where we could be free and know love. But that promise has not been fulfilled. Many females are still confused, wondering about the place of love in our lives. Many of us have been afraid to acknowledge that "love matters," for fear we will be despised and shamed by women who have come to power within patriarchy by closing off emotions, by becoming like the patriarchal men we once critiqued as cold and hard-hearted. Power feminism is just another scam in which women get to play patriarchs and pretend that the power we seek and gain liberates us. Because we did not create a grand body of work that would have taught girls and women new and visionary ways to think about love, we witness the rise of a generation of females in our late twenties and early thirties who see any longing for love as weakness, who focus our sights solely on gaining power.

Patriarchy has always seen love as women's work, degraded and devalued labor. And it has not cared when women failed to learn how to love, for patriarchal men have been the most willing to substitute care for love, submission for respect. We did not need a feminist movement to let us know that females are more likely to be concerned with relationships, connection, and community than are males. Patriarchy trains us for this role. We do need a feminist movement to remind us again and again that love cannot exist in a context of domination, that the love we seek cannot be found as long as we are bound and not free.

In my first book on the subject, *All About Love: New Visions,* I was careful to state again and again that women are not inherently more loving than men but that we are encouraged to learn how to love. That encouragement has been the catalyst for women to seek love, to look hard and long at the practice of love. And to confront our fears of not being loving, of not being loved enough. The women in our culture who have the most to teach everyone about the nature of love are the generation of females who learned through feminist struggle and feminist-based therapy that self-love was the key to finding and knowing love.

We, women who love, are among a generation of women who moved beyond the patriarchal paradigms to find ourselves. The journey to true selfhood demanded of us the invention of a new world, one in which we courageously dared to rebirth the girl within and welcome her into life, into a world where she is born valued, loved, and eternally worthy. Loving that girl within has healed the woundedness that often led us to search for love in all the wrong places. Midlife for many of us has been the fabulous moment of pause where we begin to contemplate the true meaning of love in our lives. We begin to see clearly how much love matters, not the old patriarchal versions of "love" but a deeper understanding of love as a transformational force demanding of each individual accountability and responsibility for nurturing our spiritual growth.

We bear witness to the truth that no female can find freedom without first finding her way to love. Our search for love has led us to understand fully the meaning of communion. In *The Eros of Everyday Life,* Susan Griffin writes, "The wish for communion exists in the body. It is not for strategic reasons alone that gathering together has been at the heart of every movement for social change. . . . These meetings were in themselves the realizations of a desire that is at the core of human imaginings, the desire to locate ourselves in community, to make our survival a shared effort, to experience a palpable reverence in our connections with each other and the earth that sustains us." The communion in love our souls seek is the most heroic and divine quest any human can take.

That females are born into a patriarchal world, which first invites us to make the journey to love and then places barriers in our way, is one of life's ongoing tragedies. The time has come for female elders to rescue girls and young women, to offer them a vision of love that will sustain them on their journey. To seek love as a quest for the true self liberates. All females who dare to follow our hearts to find such love are entering a cultural revolution that restores our souls and allows us to see clearly the value and meaning of love in our lives. While romantic love is a crucial part of this journey, it is no longer deemed all that matters; rather, it is an aspect of our overall work to create loving bonds, circles of love that nurture and sustain collective female well-being.

Communion: The Female Search for Love shares our struggle to know true love and our triumphs. Gathering together wisdom gleaned from women who have come to know love in midlife, women who often wandered lost in a desert of the heart through most of our teen years and on into our late twenties, *Communion* lets us hear the knowledge of women over thirty and beyond who as seekers on love's path discovered along the way new visions, healing insights, and remembered rapture.

This book is testimony, a celebration of the joy women find when we restore the search for love to its rightful, heroic place at the center of our lives. We long to be loved and we long to be free. *Communion* tells us how we fulfill that longing. Sharing the pain, the struggle, the work women do to overcome our fear of abandonment and of loss, the ways we push past the wounded passion to open our hearts, *Communion* urges us to come again and again to the place where we can know joy, to come and celebrate, to join the circle of love.

communion

One

---

aging to love, loving to age

E VERY day I talk to women about love and aging. It's an over-forty thing to do. The exciting news is this: Everyone agrees that aging is more fun than it has ever been before. It has its joys and delights. It also has its problems. What's new for many women is that the problems don't always get us down. And if they do, we don't stay down— we pick ourselves up and start over. This is part of the magic, the power and pleasure of midlife. Even though trashing feminism has become as commonplace as chatting about the weather, we all owe feminism, the women's liberation movement, women's lib—whatever you call it. It helped change how women see aging. Many of us feel better about aging because the old scripts that told us life ends at thirty or forty, that we turn into sexless zombies who bitch bitch bitch all the time and make everyone around us miserable were thrown away. So it does not matter that feminist movement has its faults—it helped everyone let these scripts go. And I do mean everyone.

We have changed our ways of thinking about aging and we have changed our ways of thinking about love. When the world started changing for women because of feminist movement and a lot became more equal than it ever had been, for a time it was only women who had been allowed a taste of power—class privilege or education or extra-special-hard-to-ignore-gifts—who most "got it" and "got with it." These women were among the feminist avant-garde. Often they had exceptional advantages or were over-achievers. While feminism helped these women soar, it often failed to change in any way the lives of masses of ordinary women. Many advantages gained by women's lib did not trickle down, but the stuff around aging did. By challenging sexist ways of thinking about the body, feminism offered new standards of beauty, telling us plump bodies were luscious and big bellies sublime, that hair hanging under our arms and covering our legs was allur-ing. It created new possibilities of self-actualization in both our work lives and our intimate lives.

As women have changed our minds about aging, no longer seeing it as negative, we have begun to think differ-ently about the meaning of love in midlife. Beth Bena-tovich's collection of interviews *What We Know So Far:*

Wisdom Among Women, offers powerful testimony affirming this fact. With prophetic insight, writer Erica Jong declares, "I believe that this is a moment of history in which we are engaged in a kind of spiritual revolution— the kind of revolution that creates pathfinders. . . . Older women are again being accorded their ancient role as prophetesses and advisors. . . . That's the great transformation that's happening again in our time. In looking to things other than the body beautiful for inspiration, we're being forced to redefine the second half of our lives, to become pathfinders." Difficulties still abound for aging women. What's most changed is the constructive way women of all ages, classes, and ethnicities cope with these difficulties. Open, honest conversations about the myriad ways empty-nest syndrome, the death of parents or a spouse, and/or the deeply tragic death of a child all create psychological havoc in our lives have helped. Our talk of this suffering would be stale and commonplace, were it not for all the creative ways women are attending to the issue of aging both in midlife and in the postsixty years. The courage to choose adventure is the ingredient that exists in women's lives today that was there for most women before the contemporary feminist movement. Contrast the women who suffered breast cancer silently with the women today who speak out, who proudly and lovingly claim their bodies intact, whole, and beautiful after surgical removals. Poet Deena Metzger boldly proclaims the beauty of the one-breasted woman on a poster. Theorist Zillah Eisenstein tells all about breast cancer, her personal story, in *Man-made Breast Cancers*. In these ways women in midlife are changing the world.

In the exciting world of women I was raised in—an extended family with lots of great-grandmothers, grandmothers, great-aunts, aunts, daughters, and their children—I learned early that aging would be full of delight. Women around us talked about the prime of their life as though it was indeed the promised land. Like beautiful snakes, they were going to reach their prime, boldly shed their skin, and acquire another—this one more powerful and beautiful than all the rest. Something in them was going to be resurrected. They were going to be born again and have another chance. These were poor women born into a world without adequate birth control, a world where having an abortion could end one's life, psychologically or physically. They were women who saw menopause as a rite of passage in which they would move from slavery to freedom. Until then they often felt trapped. This feeling of being trapped was one they shared with women across class. Even women who were solitary, celibate, and quite able to manage economically lived with the ever-present fearful possibility that all that could be changed by sexual coercion. In their world, once a woman was no longer able to bear children, she was just freer—midlife, the magic time.

Oh, how I was filled with delight when I heard Mama and her friends carry on about the joys of "the change of life." They never used the word "menopause." How intuitively sensible! Had they taken to heart medical ways of defining shifts in midlife, they might have been forced to take on board the negative implications this word would bring—the heavy weight of loss it evokes. Instead they had their own special language. A subtle, seductive, mysterious, celebratory way of talking about changes in midlife emanated from them. Like a perfumed mist whose scent has followed and haunted me, it touches me now. I have arrived. I am receiving the signs. I am in the midst of change.

To Mama, her friends, and lots of other women she would never know, the approach of midlife was exciting because it meant that they were no longer compelled to spend all their time taking care of others. They were finally to have time for themselves. The absence of free time—time spent doing nothing—had plagued them all their lives. And they looked forward to days when time would hang heavy on their hands. Days when they could think about play and rest and forget about work. Listening to Mama and her friends, I never thought about what I wanted my life to be like in midlife; I just accepted on blind faith, with absolute trust, the conviction that it would be sweeter than it had been before. Even if the before was sweet, midlife would be sweeter still. I did not know then that midlife would also be a time to rethink everything I had learned about the nature of women and love.

Most writing by women on midlife talks about menopause as though that's the only "happening" event. Not true. There are so many happening events it's hard to keep track of them all. From day one, when woman hit Earth, she has been the heartbeat of all happening events, except that most of those events were not arranged by her or for her pleasure. Much of what makes midlife magical for women now is that we are the ones making the arrangements—inventing our time and our way. For most of our lives women have followed the path of love set for us by patriarchal pathfinders. Despite our disappointments and heartaches, we have gone along with the program and accepted without challenge and critique the notion that love can exist in a context of domination. A feminist movement and many heartaches later, more women than ever before now know that love and domination do not go together—that if one is present, the other will be absent. For some of us this has caused more heartache. Since domination is still the primary order of the day, women, especially women who desire to be in partnerships with men, want to know how to love and be loved. That's one of the big questions this book answers.

When I first talked with women about writing this book, the most frequently asked question was whether or not love was as important to women in midlife as it was when we were younger. There are so many women I talked with who, like me, never thought about midlife, so many of us who thought we would be dead before the age of thirty. Our reasons for thinking this were rooted in tremendous fears about growing up, about becoming grown women. We wanted to be girls forever. As girls we felt we had power. We were strong and fierce and sure of ourselves. Somehow, as we made our entrance into the realm of young womanhood, we began to lose power. Fascinating research on girlhood is happening these days. It confirms that young girls often feel strong, courageous, highly creative, and powerful until they begin to receive undermining sexist messages that encourage them to conform to conventional notions of femininity. To conform they have to give up power.

Giving up power has been what aging has traditionally felt like for most women. And with the loss of those feelings of power came the fear that we would be forever abandoned, unloved. Now midlife and thereafter has become not only a time to reclaim power but also a time to know real love at last. More than ever before, women talk about the difficulties of being powerful in a world that has changed a lot but that still remains patriarchal. Hence we have enormous freedom in a world that is not yet fully accepting of our freedom. This fact creates new issues, ones that most women in the past did not face. Think, for example, about how many of our parents remained or remain in marriages of more than fifty years where the woman is miserable and unhappy. Yet the world they were raised in told them this was a woman's destiny. Today masses of women—women who would never call themselves feminists, who may not even feel that their lives have been in any way affected by a feminist movement— are empowered to leave relationships when they are terrorized, or miserable, or maybe not treated poorly in any way but are merely unloved. Leaving these bonds opens up the possibility that they may know love in their lifetime. The older stay-married-forever generation were and often are cynical about love.

I can still remember the pain my mother expressed at a time in her life when my father was being particularly unkind. He had always been a womanizer, but now his behavior had become just plain crazy and terroristic. They had been married for close to twenty years at that time, and I was about to finish high school. I remember urging Mama with all the hubris and wild courage of late-sixties adolescence to leave Dad. And I have never forgotten the sad and weary look on her face when she turned to me, saying in the smallest voice, "Who would want me?" With pure adolescent wonder, I was astounded by this response; I saw my mother as the most marvelous being. I demanded to know, "What on earth do you mean?" In a sad and tremulous voice she explained that she was already over the hill, that she had lots of children, that men did not desire women like that. This was one of the most painful lessons about love and heartache I learned as a girl in the bosom of patriarchy.

It warms my heart that women today, even those who may feel trapped in longtime marriages where they are unhappy, at least know that there are ways out, that there is still a world out there that desires their presence, their being. Even if an individual woman may not believe this is true for herself, she sees examples of this truth in the lives of other women in the culture. That's crucial. She has a model for change whether she chooses to make changes or not. The fact that many women now openly choose partners from both sexes means that aging females have a body of individuals with shared experiences who are seeking to share companionship, whether sexual or not, women who are seeking to know love.

A child of the fifties, I was born into a world that believed a woman should marry and stay married forever. In those days everyone I knew believed in the words "until death do us part." I was also born into a world where we went to church every Sunday and took the Scriptures seriously. However, by the time I reached my late teens—toward the end of the sixties—everything had been called into question: the legitimacy of marriage, the significance of the church. It was a time of great rebellion. Suddenly the world was rocked. Nothing was stable anymore. And I was totally "into" defiance. At the same time I was reluctant to give up all the values of my upbringing, so I tried to juggle worlds. I would give up on state-legitimized marriage, but I would hold on to my belief in the importance of commitment and constancy. I would not be seeking a husband, but I did want a lifetime companion. I rejected the notion of falling in love because it implied a lack of choice and reason, embracing the vision of love as'an act of choice and will.

Contemporary feminist movement had taught me to question notions of love that encouraged women to be victims or to masochistically subordinate ourselves to terrorizing, patriarchal men. It taught me that I did not necessarily need to place all my longing for companionship in the direction of men—that women were also a romantic option. Now, this was heady stuff for a Southern Baptist girl raised in a strict household, but I was taking it all in and trying to make necessary adjustments. My strategy for a happy life consisted of a plan to keep the good stuff from the old ways and blend it with the best of the new stuff coming in. While this strategy made for good theory, it was hard practice. And lots of stuff failed. The failure hurt most when it came to love.

From the outset, radical feminism encouraged women to question our obsession with love. In extreme cases individual women activists urged us to forget love and get into power. Love was for victims; power was for victors. Shamelessly, I clung to the visions of fulfillment in romantic love that had been imprinted on my girlhood consciousness. As a girl, I was enthralled when Ken was created to go along with Barbie. Now I could really play house. And even when feminism entered every pore of my sixteen-year-old body, I still wanted and believed in the idea of a happily-ever-after union for Barbie and Ken—for me and my chosen love.

Despite more than twenty years as a feminist thinker and activist, my obsession with love is as keen as it was when I first introduced my new Ken doll to Barbie. It was indeed an arranged marriage. With Barbie and Ken in hand, I could create a world of sustained love, a world where romantic union opened the heart and uplifted the spirit. I could create paradise. The fantasies of true love and perfect union I offered to Barbie and Ken laid the groundwork for my own quest for love. I lived in a world where my maternal grandparents were married for almost eighty years, where my parents were clearly planning to be together forever (although it was obvious to me even when I was a young child that they and couples like them were not necessarily fulfilled in love). I was obsessed with the question of fulfillment. I wanted to understand how to make love work.

This desire to understand and know love followed me from girlhood into womanhood; it was the ruling passion of my life. As I matured emotionally, the nature of that obsession changed. After feminist conversion, my thinking about love was no longer heterosexist the way it was before feminism. I begin to realize that the paths to love are many and the way of loving is one. And more than ever I knew it was possible for women to know love's delight throughout our lives. That's why I wanted to write a more personal book about women's quest for love, especially the meaning of that quest in midlife.

My first book, *All About Love: New Visions,* was a more general discussion of the meaning and practice of love in our lives. This book is a more personal discussion of the ways my thinking about love changed in midlife. Exploring my own quest for true love, I look at the ways women's lives have been forever altered by the impact of feminist movement, the way it opened up avenues that had always been closed for social equality with men. Women have greater freedom than ever before, and yet it is not clear whether that freedom has given us greater access to true love. It is not clear how that freedom has changed the nature of romance and partnership. Some of us have been married or remain in lifelong marriages and/or partnerships. Many of us are economically self-sufficient. Many of us are childless. More than ever before, there are many single women approaching midlife alone. Our longing for companions, for love, is rarely talked about in any way that realistically articulates the nature of our lives.

Until recently there has been little discussion of our fate when it comes to romantic love and partnership, other than the more commonly known notion that any single woman over thirty who is heterosexual is more likely to be alone forever. And God forbid she reaches forty without having found a man. When mass media seized on this notion, using it as propaganda to strike fear in the hearts of women, it was a subtle, indirect form of antifeminist back-lash. For those of us who were focusing more on attaining higher education, building careers, and—let's face it—"making some money" so that we could be in charge of our economic lives, being bombarded with messages telling us we were more likely to die in airplane crashes than to find a mate was nothing short of a warning. In the popular movie *Sleepless in Seattle*, everyone in the life of the char-acter played by Meg Ryan encourages her to feel worried and panicked because she is not married. Pondering the statistics that suggest she will not find love, she frets about her otherwise happy life. As a threat, these statistics served to warn women that we'd better get back to focusing on the business of getting and keeping a man—that this above all else should be our primary concern.

Now, when this dire warning struck my life, I was strug-gling with whether or not I should leave the man in my life. We had been together for more than ten years, but I was simply not satisfied. He was not committed to per-sonal growth or emotional openness. While he supported equality in the workforce, in our intimate lives he saw me as there primarily to serve his sexual needs. Like many women, I heeded the warning that I might never find another partner. Among other fears, it probably served to keep me in the relationship longer than I should have been. Ultimately, my fears were not as important as my longing for freedom, self-actualization, love. To me, leaving this relationship was not about giving up on love; it was the gesture that would set me free to really search for love— the gesture that would allow me to love again. And so I left. And leaving felt good. I was never going to know love in that relationship. Leaving it opened up the possibility of finding love.

Love should be as important to women in midlife as it was to us when we were girls, when we were wide-eyed teenagers looking for true love and perfect union. We are still looking. Some of us have found the love we longed for. The magic of midlife is that many of us now know more about the meaning of love; we know more about what it means to love and be loved. We are more experienced.

Most of us have suffered heartache. Pain has opened us up—given us the opportunity to learn from our suffering— to make ourselves ready for the love that is promised. We know love is there. Some of us are still waiting. We know we will love again. And when we love, we know love will last. Significantly, we know, having learned through much trial and error, that true love begins with self-love. And that time and time again our search for love brings us back to the place where we started, back to our own heart's mirror, where we can look upon our female selves with love and be renewed.

Feminist critiques of love made it difficult for progressive, powerful women to speak about the place of love in our lives. This silence has undermined the freedom of all females to be fully self-actualized, which women's liberation first championed. While feminist thinkers and activists were right to rip apart and throw away outmoded, patriarchal ways of thinking about love and romance, girls and women still need to fill the gap with new liberatory visions full of hope and promise. Without these new visions to serve as guides and maps, the path to love remains difficult to find and the search for love leaves us unfulfilled and lacking. Women, along with the culture as a whole, need constructive visions of redemptive love. We need to return to love and proclaim its transformative power.

Two

love's proper place

M Y mother never talked about love. She and her sisters were good-looking women who liked having a good time. They married young, and they had babies. Marriage was more important than love. Love could lead you astray. Marriage was the safe place—a place where women could bury dreams and pretend, create a make-believe world and remain there forever. Even before my teen years I knew that I did not want to marry. I had taken a close look at my parents' marriage and decided it was not for me. Or, as I remember confidently putting it to my mother in the midst of a quarrel, "I am never going to marry. I'm never letting any man tell me what to do." Of course, this was my indirect way of challenging her about the way she bowed down to Dad's every whim.

Like all the other women of her generation, women who married in the late forties and early fifties, my mother believed that it was a woman's place to stand behind and by her man. It was her place to obey his will and to meet his every need. In return he would protect and provide. These beliefs were upheld by Scripture and church, by school and community, and by the women's magazines she liked so much. They probably would have had a greater impact on my consciousness had I not been more fascinated by the relationship between my maternal grandmother, Baba, and my grandfather, Daddy Gus. They did not talk about love, either. They had been married forever. And as kids we were fascinated by their bond because we knew they had separate rooms. Our parents never wanted to explain to us why they did not sleep together, but they (our old and talkative grandparents) were always eager to tell all. Baba made no bones about the fact that she could not stand the constant smell of tobacco, and he—our granddaddy—reeked of tobacco. He rolled his own smokes, so there was always loose tobacco about, on his dresser, in his pockets. Daddy Gus was even more adamant that sleeping by oneself made more sense than sleeping with someone else, 'cause you had your bed and your room just the way you liked it. That's what I remember most about my grandparents. Their rooms expressed separate and unique personalities. They taught me by example that it was possible to be married and still keep your own identity.

In their house Baba ruled. Watching her take control of home and hearth, we learned that men were not always in charge. Daddy Gus was a laid-back man, kind and gentle. Baba was a take-charge, confrontational, lay-down-the-rules type; she liked wielding power, and she could be cruel. As a small girl, I knew that my father disapproved of their reversal of traditional gender roles. He believed that in a proper family the man would always be the undisputed head of the household. In our home he was the patriarch. His word was law. Power—not love—seemed to be the underlying theme of daily life in both these households. Yet I could see early on that Baba's household, this world where a woman ruled, was a kinder, gentler place than the world of my parents' marriage. While my grandparents had a peaceful bond, tension and conflict characterized Mom and Dad's relationship. I decided very young that if marriage was to be this power struggle with one person on top and another on the bottom, I wanted no part of it. I lost interest in marriage at an early age, but this loss merely intensified my desire to search for and find a love that would be more vital than the will to power.

My ideas about love also came from books and television. As a girl of the fifties I was taught that a woman's place was in the home. That her destiny was to be a good homemaker, to care for husband and family in sickness and in health without complaint. In her role as caregiver she was also responsible for everyone else's happiness. It was her job to create emotional well-being. She did that by meeting everyone's needs. In childhood I saw how hard our mother worked to accomplish all these tasks. We (her children) admired her ability to organize, to do everything with grace, skill, and beauty. She delivered the goods. While Dad was preoccupied with work and his pleasure, she satisfied our hearts' desires.

Despite her generosity and power, all her gifts were taken for granted. There were no rewards. Our dad, "the patriarch," always found fault. The perfection we saw in her was never enough for him. She was always working overtime to please. It wore her out. Bone weary, she tried to assert herself in midlife by going against my father's wishes and working outside the home. Even then he found ways to undermine her newly achieved independence. This has happened to many married women who entered the workforce in midlife hoping to gain greater economic self-sufficiency and freedom but found these hopes dashed when husbands either appropriated their earnings or deducted the amount the women earned from the household expenses the men once contributed. Yet even when women, like my mother, did not find self-sufficiency and economic freedom in the workforce, they often found their self-esteem boosted. And that boost made a difference, however relative, in their daily lives. By the time I reached my sweet-sixteen year, I had witnessed enough of Mama's weariness to know this was not for me. I would not be a subordinated wife or a homemaker.

And the only way out of that role for a working-class girl was education. The only career that women entered in our world if they did not marry was teaching. More than anything, I loved reading books as a girl and wanted to write them. Countless biographies by women reveal that girl children witnessing a mother's suffering at the hands of male tyrants—fathers, brothers, and/or husbands—are deeply, traumatically affected. Not only do we want to rescue our mothers but also we want to change our destiny so we will never suffer the way they did or do. Determined to invent my fate, I turned away from acceptable female roles.

Even before I knew there was a women's liberation movement, I rebelled against conventional expectations. When I let the world know that I wanted to be a writer, that I had no intention of being a wife or mother, my family responded with horror. They believed that satan was speaking through me. In their belief system it just wasn't natural for any female not to desire home and family, to refuse to be obsessed with marriage. To go against these desires was to go against God; it marked me as a sinner— one of the lost.

Even though I accepted my lost-girl identity, I felt I was a freak of nature. I had not chosen this identity; it had been imposed on me by unseen forces. I could not help the fact that I longed for a good book more than I longed to hold hands with Oscar Brewer. I accepted my fate even though it caused me suffering. Religiously, my parents tried to pull me out of books. They shamed. They humiliated. They punished. Those books were ruining me, giving me too many ideas and too much mouth—all things that destroy a woman's ability to be a good homemaker. In the presence of our father, our mother affirmed these beliefs. However, when he was gone, in the daytime shade of our everyday life, when he was at work, she encouraged reading. She talked about her schoolgirl days, her longing to be a writer. This split in her personality was the one space of private rebellion against patriarchy. It was the space where she revealed her deep disappointment in marriage. It had not proven to be a safe place where she was cherished, taken care of, protected, and loved. Yet at the end of the day, in the nighttime gloom, when Daddy came home, she was still a fifties mom.

And I remained a freak of nature—one of those unnatural females who was trying to resist the notion of biology as destiny. In those days the so-called great psychologists had confirmed that we could not escape. That it was normal for woman to be passive. That any desire for agency on her part was pathological. She should be fulfilled with and through her man. A woman who desired something more was a demon destroyer, crazy and castrating. With the appropriate amount of shame and self-loathing, I accepted my fate even as I secretly believed I could change it. I believed I could and would find a mate who would love me just as I was. I could and would have it all: my ideas, books, writing, and love. The only world that affirmed that this was indeed possible was the world of books.

Books helped me to separate marriage and love. I gave up on marriage as a girl, but I believed wholeheartedly in an all-powerful redemptive love. True love and perfect union came into my world through fairy tales and then, later, romances. From these imaginative tales I learned it was possible to find a soul mate and with that partner heal the wounds of childhood. Cinderella was the prime example. While fate had led her to be the victim of pain and injustice, she was rescued by love. Like Snow White, Rapunzel, and all the other storybook heroines who were lost but found their way home, I believed I would be rescued from the lovelessness of my childhood. Finding love would heal my wounds.

Later, when I read the Victorians, my conviction that love would rescue me intensified. Jo's fate in *Little Women* was testimony that life could be different, that love would prevail. While she does not end up with the man of her dreams, she marries a perfect partner for her, one who values her intellect. *Jane Eyre* was proof that one could come out of the suffering of childhood and abuse to find ones self-admired, desired, loved. I alternated between reading the great classical literature of love and cheap romances. Indeed, back in the day when Mills & Boon first published books that would later become Harlequin Romances, most of the stories were about working-class females coming through hardship and finding as their reward a love relationship with a powerful and oftentimes, but not always, wealthy man. Central to these plots was the insistence that the heroic male worship and adore the women in his life. No violence or domestic abuse existed in this world of poor and working-class women finding love.

I was not alone in believing in the transformative power of love. Even normal girls who longed for marriage and family believed that they would enter these portals through the gates of romantic love. The prevailing psychological mores of the fifties sanctioned our innocent belief that we would find ourselves in and through love. The men we loved would redeem and rescue us. We were willing to give all to love because we believed love would return that all. And in the case of those of us who were freaks of nature, who were not "naturally" obsessed with getting and keeping a man, love was all the more important. It was our only hope of salvation.

My early loves were always unobtainable "bad" boys. While I could attract their attention in the way nerdy, smart, cute girls fascinate, I could never hold it long, since I failed to deliver the adoration of maleness and the phallus that really mattered. I was not the kind of girl a boy could sweet-talk and seduce. Sexual fantasies of going all the way were the stuff of my dream life, but in reality all the boys I knew were deathly afraid of my father. If they left me intact, spared me seduction or date rape in the backseat of cars—often the plight of an innocent, smart, virginal girl—it was only because they feared the silent patriarch (my father—Mr. Veodis), who they believed would violently avenge any assault on his female property. The only high school love I had that was in any way sustained was with Skipper, a lanky athlete two years my junior, tall for his age. Initially, I was teased for seeing a younger boy. I chose Skipper because he liked the fact that I was smart. My parents were pleased because there was at last concrete proof that I was "normal." Choosing Skipper meant there was hope for me. I wish I could say my choice was a sign of courage. Instead I feared not being "normal." As a consequence, whenever I felt interest in a male, I pursued the connection with great passion. Mostly, males of all ages aroused in me little curiosity and much fear. I had been taught to fear maleness, the power of the father to punish and the power of men to ruin and rape.

My father spoke directly to me about men. Whenever one of my sisters wanted to date someone deemed unacceptable, he would testify to his knowledge of men, telling us that he knew "what men were really like," and we did not need to find out. The one lesson he taught us about men that lasted was that real men were to be feared. We feared him. And therefore never truly had the opportunity to know him, either to give him love or to know his love. He protected and provided. To demand that he take notice of us beyond that was to invite trouble. Up until I left home, I lost all battles with my father. His word was law. It was impossible to love him or to feel his love. He was the patriarch who inspired fear, not love. The last battle between my father and me occurred over my desire to attend Stanford University, which was far from our working class Kentucky home, all the way in California, a strange and sinful place. Even though I had placed all my dreams at my mother's feet, since she was both the interpreter of dreams and the magician of desire who could make dreams come true, it was my father, the silent one who had not been "in" on discussions about college, who decided I could not go. California was too far away. He never spoke a word to me about college. Since his word was law, his decision was final. Mom was his messenger. At first I accepted the verdict, shedding tears of rage and throwing my acceptance letter into the wastebasket. Then something in me rebelled.

I felt in my soul that this was my chance and I needed to take it. I defied the will of the father. And I did not die. Rebelliously, I announced that I was going to Stanford. I never knew what my father thought about my decision. When I went away to college, my mother stood alone at the bus stop waving good-bye and wishing me well.

Leaving home merely heightened my sense of being a lost soul in this world, a wanderer in search of home. Finding home was synonymous in my mind with finding love. I arrived at Stanford in the wake of the late-sixties rebellion against the war in Vietnam. Rebellion was the order of the day. Black-power advocates were daring everyone to be militantly antiracist; the invention and widespread use of the birth-control pill had made sexual liberation commonplace; and the feminist movement was changing everything about women's lives. And there I was, a naive Kentucky girl trying to find my way home.

The journey was both adventurous and frightening. I, like many of my female Stanford peers, was full of contradictions. I wanted to find my own identity and be autonomous at the same time that I wanted to find a mate who would rescue me, who would provide and protect. Of course I wanted to be able to provide for myself. Just in case that did not happen, I wanted the luxury of backup. I was not a free spirit. I wanted to blend old-fashioned values learned at home—which cautioned me to be conservative, take care, and be responsible—with New Age spirituality and radical ideas of freedom and choice. No matter how much I might have longed to free myself from a sense of responsibility to the collective good, to family and community, I was psychically bound. I had the strength to rebel, but I did not have the strength to let go. I was, like generations of women before me, split, torn between two competing identities—the longing to be the liberated, independent, sexually free woman and the desire to settle down and be domesticated. Whereas my mother and her generation had felt torn between their longing to be good wives and mothers and the desire for unique self-expression, I was torn between my desire to follow the dictates of my inner self and my distrust of that self.

While I had chosen to adopt the persona of the rebellious girl, the crazy one—and it seemed like a small price to pay for being able to be in touch with my longing to create, to know myself and the world—I was not prepared to face that world alone. I simply did not have the necessary survival skills. Despite eating problems (I often ending up at student health), sleepless nights, and bouts of intense depression, I doggedly pursued my own way. I wanted to be self-actualized. When being "lost" was too great a burden for my spirit, I searched for love—for a partner who would help me in the quest to sustain myself and give me the necessary courage to go on.

This struggle to find support for being a rebellious female who resists sexist norms is still faced by young women today. To define themselves against the tyranny of sexist devaluation, today's young women proudly adopt the "bitch" persona. Thirty-something and fierce Elizabeth Wurtzel declares that "the bitch persona appeals to us" because "it is the illusion of liberation, of libertine abandon." My generation of rebellious women, all of us now in our late forties and early fifties, did not want to be bitches. We wanted to be fully self-actualized, self-realized, whole. And we knew that the world was against that, against us. Our hope was that as we searched for love, we would find a partner, male or female, who would affirm this quest.

Not enough has been written about the transitional period women go through when we let go of old agendas for our lives and begin to embark on new journeys. While there is much historical and sociological writing documenting shifts that occurred in women's thinking and behavior in the late sixties and early seventies as a consequence of advanced methods of birth control and the women's liberation movement, the psychological consequences of these shifts are not articulated as clearly. Unlike a significant number of my female peers who had come from privileged class backgrounds, where either their mothers were career women or fathers supported their quest for autonomous selfhood, I and individuals like me strived alone. This heightened isolation was often the breeding ground for mental illness.

Recently I told one of my younger sisters (both of us in midlife) that I saw my first therapist (a psychiatrist) when I was eighteen. She, a therapist, wanted to know what led me to seek help. I responded by telling her, "I knew I wasn't normal. It wasn't normal to want to kill yourself. I knew I needed help. Luckily, I was a first-year college student at a women's college (before transferring to the coed world of Stanford University), where mental concerns were addressed without negative stigma. I was in the company of lots of talented, smart young women who wanted to walk on a path different from the one our parents chose for us. Our rebellion placed us at risk psychically. There was an emotional cost to not fitting in.

Those of us who suffered because we did not have enough maps to chart our journey and were not able to fully articulate our stories found solace in the writing of Sylvia Plath. She was an icon for my generation, because her experience typified the conflicts we endured or struggled with and the contradictions we were going through. We wanted to be the equals of men in every way, and we wanted to be ourselves, and we were not sure that those two journeys would take us to the same place. Though coming to womanhood in a world of incredible social equality between the sexes, Elizabeth Wurtzel is right on target in *Bitch: In Praise of Difficult Women* when she writes, "Plath is the voice of one who wants to be allowed to want—she wants the luxury of not just one desire, but many. . . . Denied the delicious nourishment of all that is happy and hopeful in what she desires, she is drained and empty, an emotional wreck. The need is a burdensome absence whose weight is so much greater than her brilliant presence: in the end, it is psychic starvation that kills her." In the early seventies, the period Plath represented in her novel *The Bell Jar,* the deepest inner conflicts of smart girls were the fear of our bodies' betraying us, the depression suffered from lack of emotional support, and the reality of there being nowhere to turn.

In my case I was caught between the image of myself as crazy, hysterical, and a freak that had been imposed on me in the patriarchal family and the image of myself as a bohemian woman writer that I had fashioned largely in the realm of fantasy. There were certainly no role models for the woman I wanted to become. For a long time Emily Dickinson's fate represented to me a realistic model for my life. By choosing to be a writer, I would be alone. Like Dickinson, I would not live alone, as no woman in my family history had ever lived alone; single women were sheltered by family and kin. Like Dickinson, I would create an alone space in the midst of patriarchal community. Even though my family at times supported my quest to acquire an education to ensure that I would get a good job, that support always ceased when they thought I was learning ideas that ran counter to the values of home and church.

When I arrived at Stanford University, eager to become an intellectual and a writer, I was not at all prepared to live away from the strict fundamentalist Christian community I had known all my life. All my freethinking had been done in the bosom of the fascist family. All my rebellion had been about small matters. And the punishments were fierce. Suddenly there were no guards, no spies, no one to come home and report to. Yet I still had to contend with the overseers in my own mind. Whether using the voice of patriarchal family or church, these internalized authorities kept me in check. These were the voices insisting that sex before marriage was sin, that it would ruin a good woman; that to choose to be smart would alienate men; that to be "too smart" would make a woman crazy. I tried to speak back to these voices in defiance, but I could never really let them go. If I experimented or ventured out, I went only so far—never all the way. Psychologically, I had been socialized within the family to fear for my mental health. Taught to believe I was just a breakdown away from being sent to a mental institution for the rest of my life, I did not trust myself or my desires.

Not yet shrewd enough to seek progressive mental-health care that would help me confront phobias and debilitating fears, I looked for love. While this search took time and energy, it never distracted my attention from academic and intellectual work. Of course, I was rescued from madness by feminist movement. Women's liberation gave focus to my quest and my longings. It validated my desire to be self-realized. Yet it did not change my yearning to find love. It helped me to put the search for love in proper perspective. It helped me to see that women within patriarchy could not depend on the love of a good man to affirm our quest for selfhood.

Ultimately, I could not count on finding love, I could

count on my mind. I looked for love, but I found freedom. And the freedom I found changed my way of thinking about the place of love in a woman's life. I began to see that the proper place for love in a woman's life was not relational love as the source but love generated in the quest for self-realization. By claiming that quest as essential, as the journey that would determine my fate, I realized that the proper place for love was as the solid foundation on which I would invent self and create a life. Uniting the search for love with the quest to be free was the crucial step. Searching for love, I found the path to freedom. Learning how to be free was the first step in learning to know love.

Three

looking for love, finding freedom

MY search for love led me to feminism. Feminist thinking freed me from the weight of the past. Breaking the isolation that had been my lot throughout my growing-up years, feminism drew to me groups of women who had similar stories to tell, women who, like me, wanted to be fully self-actualized, who wanted to end sexism, who wanted to be sexually free and heart-whole. Suddenly, we were all listening to our voices. My first women's-studies class was taught by the writer Tillie Olsen. Sharing with us memories of the pain of her own struggle as a working-class woman coping with marriage and family while trying to build a career as a writer, she offered us firsthand accounts of the sacrifices and the wounds. Her testimony stirred my soul. Reading the ending of Olsen's short story

"I Stand Here Ironing," what questing female heart could not be stirred by the mother saying of her daughter, "My wisdom came too late. She has much in her and probably nothing will come of it. She is a child of her age, of depression, of war, of fear. Let her be. So all that is in her will not bloom—but in how many does it? There is still enough left to live by. Only help her to believe—help make it so there is cause for her to believe that she is more than this dress on the ironing board, helpless before the iron?" This was Olsen's fiction. A passionate teacher in real life, she was urging us, young feminist thinkers, to blossom, to dare, to risk.

As I moved deeper and deeper into radical feminist thinking, I found there the one place where relationships between women and men were seriously discussed. In our consciousness-raising classes and intimate gatherings, we learned ways to understand the impact of patriarchal thinking on our relationships with men. Contrary to mass media's insistence that we were learning how to be man-hating, in fact we were taught to understand the ways male identity and self-actualization were usurped by patriarchal socialization. Men who oppressed women did not do so because they acted simply from the space of free will; they were in their own way agents of a system they had not put into place. Yet our compassion for patriarchy's abuse of men was not as intense as our passion for female agency and our will to gain social equality with men.

Long before there was a resurgence of New Age writing about love, women active in feminist movement made us open our eyes and examine the extent to which the very ways we thought about love—our founding narratives— were not only handed to us by men but shaped to reinforce and sustain male domination. Feminist movement created a revolution in psychological thought. For the first time ever, sexist male biases in psychoanalytic theory were laid bare. Women and men who listened to feminist thinkers heard the way conventional theories were shaped to sustain patriarchal assumptions, heard the demands for change, and listened as new theories about female development were brought to light.

Ultimately, heterosexuality was called into question. Slogans like "Scratch his love, and you'll find your fear," "Sleeping with the enemy," and "Feminism is the theory and lesbianism the practice" were popularized. Theorist Marilyn Frye would write, "There is so much pressure on women to be heterosexual, and this pressure is both so pervasive and so completely denied, that I think heterosexuality cannot come naturally to many women. . . . I think that most women have to be coerced into heterosexuality. I would like heterosexual women to consider this proposition, seriously. . . . I would like heterosexual women to be as actively curious about how and why and when they became heterosexual as I have been about how and why and when I became a Lesbian." This questioning did not occur because women active in feminist movement were man-hating. It was a direct response to the reality that when individual women attempted to share feminist thinking and practice with men in their lives, they met strong opposition. Most men did not want to give up the privileges accorded them by patriarchy. If men were not willing to embrace and advocate feminist politics, if they were committed to sexist hierarchy, then they did constitute a threat to the movement; they were positioning themselves as the enemy. Logically, women responded to this threat by calling attention to the reality that it was possible to live a life without men at the center—one wherein women would not need to bow down to male demands.

No doubt individual feminist women who may have begun their sexual and romantic lives as heterosexuals simply grew tired of trying to convert men to their way of thinking and decided it was much easier to build sustained loving bonds with folks like themselves. In those days we passionately debated the question of whether or not it was possible for women to achieve feminist liberation in the context of intimate relationships with patriarchal men. Few men showed themselves willing to embrace feminist conversion. Women who wanted to hold on to their relationships with men while simultaneously embracing feminism were compelled to engage in endless power struggles that were no longer the lot of women who simply walked away from men.

Ideas about love handed down to us by patriarchal narratives had told us again and again that it was the
woman's place to be the nurturer and the caregiver. Feminist thinking shook us to our core, because it told us this
was just nonsense. That what we were hearing in these
narratives was not the rhetoric of love at all but the ideology of domination. Men had taken the idea of love and
refashioned it to serve their own ends. Radical feminism
not only urged women to examine our notions of love, it
encouraged us to forget about love.

At the same time that I embraced radical feminism, I
met the man with whom I intended to spend the rest of my
life. Not once did I imagine that I had fallen in love. Liberated women did not "fall in love," we *chose* to love—that
was different from *falling* in love. Choosing meant that we
exercised will, power, and agency. Falling implied a loss of
power, the possibility of victimhood. I never imagined he
was the man of my dreams. In fact, I had never been able
to make the man of my dreams assume a concrete form,
one that could be applied to a real-life partner. With all the
hubris of my newfound feminism, I assumed he would
become the man of my dreams if I just offered a blueprint.
At the very end of the sixties and the beginning of the seventies, bold, brilliant, brassy, beautiful young women who
were into feminism and sexual liberation believed we
could demand of men not only that they recognize that we
were their equals in bed and out but that they should

accept that we were perhaps sexually superior, that it was essential to our identities to explore our sexualities, including involvements with women. We were not interested in monogamy, as that could possibly place us at the mercy of an individual man.

Our goal in everything was personal growth. To be fully self-actualized, we needed to sprout wings and fly all over the place. Around this time women began to declare among ourselves that "good girls go to heaven and bad girls go everywhere," and there was not a radical feminist in sight who did not believe that she was a "bad" girl. New Age spirituality was big. And we were, as Ntozake Shange would later proclaim in her play *For Colored Girls Who Have Considered Suicide / When the Rainbow Is Enuf,* finding God in ourselves "and loving Her fiercely."

There is no progressive woman I know who lived through this time and underwent the changes I am talking about who did not feel born again. We lived our lives with intensity, inspired by a lust for change that was so powerful and fierce it was awesome. Our parents did not know what to do with us. Universities that had been primarily "for men only" did not know what to do when the best and brightest were girls, and sexy girls at that. Truly, this was a time of cultural revolution. Boundaries of race, gender, and class were being crossed. We all wanted to be changed utterly by all these movements for social justice.

And at the heart of all this change was a demand that we rethink the politics of heterosexual love and romance.

To many of us, "the dawning of the Age of Aquarius" meant not only that we would proclaim love and study war no more but that the love we proclaimed would be a love centered in sharing and mutuality. Women would no longer be the sole nurturers and caregivers; men would do their part. Men would no longer be burdened with the role of protector and provider; women would enter the workforce as equals and take self-defense classes and be able to protect ourselves. Men could assume the role of unemployed homemaker if that was their choice. Their value would no longer be determined by the weight of their paycheck. Reproductive rights would be the order of the day, and parenting would be above all a choice; babies would be born because they were wanted and not because they were mistakes that could not be corrected. Marriage as sanctioned by the state was an unnecessary institution; commitment and constancy would emerge as dictates of the heart and not by court orders and demands. Same-sex love would be respected and valued. Whether one was born gay or became gay, it was all "right on."

In this magic moment, some of the young men in our lives really did try to change in order to meet our demands. When changes came through endless conflict and struggle, that was seen as merely the nature of revolution. And feminism was making revolution. When we attempted to actualize our utopian longings in the concrete space of real life, everything was not fun and games, and justice did not always prevail. I had chosen a male partner seven years older than myself. We attended the same classes, ones that were open to graduate and undergraduate students. When he got better grades, we blamed it on the patriarchal system. It was not his fault. He willingly assumed his share of the chores—cooking, cleaning, and taking care of the household. He championed the rights of women in the workplace and believed we should get equal pay for equal work. He championed my intellectual growth, serving as a mentor. Our most intense power struggles took place in the bedroom. He still believed that women should "service" male desire. He, of course, objected to the use of the word "service" and preferred "respond to." I demanded that we use the word "service." I wanted him to understand that I was not responsible for his sexual desires. And if his dick was hard and he needed to put it someplace to seek satisfaction, then he had to find the place. He could not assume that my body was territory he could occupy at will.

Like all my female buddies, I was into sex and sexual liberation. Radical feminism urged us to see our bodies as ourselves and to let no one make us into territory or property. In our consciousness-raising groups, in bed with lesbian women who had made the choice never or no longer to deal with men, we were interrogated. We were sleeping with the enemy, and our activist sisters wanted to know if we were surrendering in the bedroom or if we were standing strong, claiming our sexual agency. In actuality, those of us who were sleeping with men, choosing them as primary partners, were losing the war in the bedroom. Men celebrated our sexual liberation—our willingness to freely give and enjoy blow jobs and group sex, our willingness to experiment with anal penetration—but ultimately many males revolted when we stated that our bodies were territories that they could not occupy at will. Men who were ready for female sexual liberation if it meant free pussy, no strings attached, were rarely ready for feminist female sexual agency. This agency gave us the right to say yes to sex, but it also empowered us to say no.

All of these issues were the subject of constant debate. Since the feminist movement had rocked our world, women who embraced the movement were constantly, critically vigilant. We attended countless groups, classes, and meetings to discuss the link between theory and practice. We were forever doing battle with the men in our lives. That battle was at its most extreme on the sexual front. I remember the look of sheer disbelief on my partner's face when I told him that he needed to understand that if I did not want to have sex for months, that was my choice, and that it should be clear that I was not responsible for meeting his sexual needs. Even though he thought I had lost my mind—that I was taking this feminist stuff too far—he agreed in principle that I was right, that real freedom for women, especially those of us in relationships with men, would mean that we (like men) would always have the right to refuse to perform sexually without backlash. If he wanted to have sex and I did not, he could either change the nature of his sexual desire, masturbate, or have sex with other people. He chose the latter.

We agreed to have an open relationship. Nonmonogamy had been celebrated by feminist women involved with men as a way out of sexual slavery. No man could imagine you were "his" property if it was always clear that you could choose at any moment to be sexual with someone else. Certainly we women were accustomed to men acting on sexual desire outside primary relationships, without female consent. Unfortunately, when women in relationships with men tried to exercise equality, we came up against barriers erected by patriarchal thinking in men's minds. Most men simply did not want to fuck with you if you had a primary relationship with another man. Or, as was often the case, they would do so only if they could consult the man and make sure he was in agreement. This practice did not affirm women's rights to control our bodies; it implied we were still the property of men. Now women were more than willing to have sex with men who were in primary partnerships (including marriage) with other women. And we did not go to those women to ask permission. We respected the right of men to choose their sexual partners. Even the men who professed to believe in "free love" held on to patriarchal notions of possessiveness when it came to sexuality. Radical heterosexual feminists who remained in relationships with men were forced to confront the truth of our lesbian sisters' insistence that men would never respect our sexual rights—that they would never love us enough to let us be free.

Men did care enough to struggle with our demands. And some cared enough to convert to feminist thinking and to change. But only a very, very few loved us—loved us all the way. And that meant respecting our sexual rights. To this day I believe that feminist debate about love and sexuality ended precisely because straight women did not want to face the reality that it was highly unlikely in patriarchal society that a majority of men would wholeheartedly embrace women's right to say no in the bedroom. Since the vast majority of heterosexual women, even those involved in radical feminist movement, were not willing to say no when they did not want to perform sexually for fear of upsetting or alienating their mates, no significant group of men ever had to rise to the occasion. While it became more acceptable for women to say no now and then, it was not acceptable to say no for any significant amount of time. An individual woman in a primary relationship with a man could not say no, because she feared there was always another woman in the background who could take her place, a woman who would never say no. When my partner and I agreed to be non-monogamous, to create a relationship where sex was not equated with love, one in which we were equally free to satisfy sexual desires if our partners were not interested, women were the group who continually encouraged him to feel that he was being cheated, that he was not with a real woman, because a real woman would be always ready and willing to satisfy his demands. Granted, these women were usually not supportive of feminist thinking.

Had feminist movement not created the social conditions for women to rethink the meaning of love, none of us would have been able to forge the new and different bonds with men that we were forging. If, as radical feminism told us, love was truly possible only between equals, to love women meant that men had to let go of their acceptance of patriarchal thinking and action. Women would not have the rights we have today if our male allies in struggle had not converted to feminist thinking. Since the sexual revolution made us all aware of the reality that there was a large population of gay men, we also embraced this constituency. This group, more so than their straight counterparts, was willing to concede power and accept sexual equality. Bonds of love between gay men and women of all sexual preferences opened up the possibility that women could turn away from patriarchal straight men and still have a sustained connection with masculine peers.

Narratives of love changed in the late sixties and early seventies. The contemporary feminist movement had put in place a new social order. The politics of heterosexual love and romance were forever changed. Women had been given a vision of mutuality—of relationships in which we would no longer be forced to be the sole nurturers and caregivers. Those of us who wanted to be fully self-actualized, to explore our creativity and develop our inner selves, no longer had to see ourselves as freaks. We could be professors or homemakers, writers or readers—feminism had given us choice. However, when it came to the subject of love, the narrative had changed, but we were still waiting to see if women and men would embrace the new narratives and love each other differently. We were disturbed and frightened by the recognition that women might find it easier to gain equality with men in the workforce and even in the bedroom but that we might still never find love. By the end of the seventies we had found freedom, but we were still looking for love. We were searching for a love that could embrace the newly invented free women we had become. Whether straight or gay, promiscuous or celibate, we were not sure how to love ourselves as free women or how to create a culture where we could be loved. We had to find a way to redefine our notion of women's liberation so it would include our right to love and be loved.

Four

---

finding balance: work and love

SEARCHING for love, I left the relationship I had been in for almost fifteen years. This common-law marriage began when I was nineteen and ended in my mid-thirties. My partner and I had not been able to fully realize the vision of mutuality, equality, and equity that had been our manifesto in the world of the late sixties and seventies. We were no longer in college. Leaving the rarefied atmosphere of progressive campus life affected many radical thinkers. Suddenly, faced with making a living in the real "white supremacist capitalist patriachal" work world, many of us began to shift our values away from the freethinking of those heady days of cultural revolution to compromise and adjust. More and more, everyone around us was becoming increasingly conservative.

The militant feminist movement, coupled with changes in the buying power of the dollar, changed the nature of the workforce. Surveys indicated that whether or not they were profeminist, more and more men supported the idea of women working outside the home. As women gained greater economic power and new freedoms, the movement began to lose its force and power. In the world outside the home, feminist success could be registered easily, but inside the home, traditional ways of doing things were making a slow and steady comeback. In the eighties, to the dismay of feminists everywhere, it soon became evident that women were doing what sociologist Arlie Hochschild called in her book of the same title "the second shift," which is to say that, increasingly, most women were working outside the home but still performing almost all the labor inside the home (child care, cooking, cleaning, and so on). Ultimately, it had been easier to create a revolution outside the home than inside. Within individual households one woman usually had to stand up against one man, as well as children, to try to convince them that they should change ingrained habits of being. This was no easy task.

I can still remember the anger and hostility at one of my sisters by her husband and children when she decided to go back to school to finish her undergraduate degree and then work toward a master's. Her husband worked in an auto plant, and felt he made enough money to provide for the family. However, my sister, like many women, felt isolated and trapped by domesticity. As the children were growing up and leaving home, she was the one who had no world outside the home. Naturally, she found this depressing. She also feared she was setting a bad example for her daughters. Being a student again and then later working outside the home gave her a new lease on life. It also meant that she was no longer present to cook and clean for everyone, to service their every need. And initially they were quite pissed off. While she persevered, it caused her considerable emotional anguish. Not only did she face emotionally alienating her family, but also she feared harming the family. Even though in time they all adjusted and found their family life enhanced by the presence of a working mom who was not always angry and depressed, for a long time they were not supportive.

There is little literature documenting what really happened when ordinary women already in patriarchal families changed their thinking and endeavored to incorporate feminist values into their family lives. This untold story would expose the failure of feminism to offer concrete guidelines showing ways to convert the family to feminist thinking. Most women had to go it alone. And many of them gave up, surrendered to the status quo, depressed and defeated.

Women's inability to achieve the same successes in the domestic household that were being achieved in the world of work actually created a different kind of rage. Many women felt betrayed by feminism. As one woman put it in the mid-eighties, "I've really been fucked over by feminism." This was a woman who had been in a longtime marriage and, because she had believed in a vision of equality, had paid her own way despite the fact that she made considerably less than her husband, yet she felt in the long run she had nothing to show for her equality—no house, no disposable income. While women agreed that work outside the home could be as much drudgery as work inside the home, almost everyone acknowledged that having a job gave a measure of independence and autonomony, increased self-esteem, and the possibility of new interests. However, only women who made large incomes were truly liberated by work. These were the women who did not have to work "the second shift" when they returned home, as they could hire caregivers: a cook, a housekeeper, a nanny, and so on. Partnered women who made smaller incomes found that it was the man in the house who benefited most from these changes. He had less economic pressure and less responsibility. Often, women felt so guilty about working outside that they worked even harder to create the "perfect" home. Also, working outside the home did not mean that women were no longer financially dependent on men. In many cases men who previously contributed income to the household held on to their money, and women's wages were spent for the household, thus eliminating the possibility that her newly gained economic clout would translate into actual freedom and power to demand equality or escape male domination. Among females, to a grave extent, single working women benefited the most from increased opportunities for women in the workforce. Newly working women with husbands and/or families often felt that life had become harder, more difficult. To them, it felt as though the feminist insistence on work as the road to freedom had been a betrayal. Their critique was justified.

They directed their rage at the feminist movement. But they also felt and sometimes expressed rage toward male partners and family. To the extent that masses of women entered the workforce without the full support and approval of males in the family, the home became even more a location for tension and conflict. Not only were masses of women entering the workforce, but also they were embracing a newfound psychological independence. This became the foundation for women to demand more from love. Contributing equally to the economic sustenance of the household gave lots of women permission to demand more of men emotionally. Prior to the large-scale entry of women into the workforce, men often claimed that working hard took too much energy, that they were drained and could not be expected to give emotionally when they came home. Now women were working, most often doing a second shift, and we were still expected to give love.

Balancing work and love, doing a fine job at both, many women began to expect more from men emotionally. When it came to the realm of heterosexual romance, we wanted to give and receive love rooted in sharing and mutuality.

At the end of the day it was infinitely easier for men to make way for women in the workforce, to do some if not an equal portion of the work at home, even to take on a more primary parenting role, than it was for them to give more emotionally. With hindsight, I can see I demanded of my partner that he give more emotionally because I did not understand what I understand now, which is the reality that he did not have more to give. He was emotionally blocked. He was shut down. We had stayed together far longer than many of our legally married counterparts. To many onlookers we came as close to having a caring, constructive, equal partnership as anyone could expect to have. Sadly, even though we went to therapy together and tried hard to save our bond, love did not prevail. Realistically, it would have taken years of psychological work for him to find the emotional space wherein he could actually give love; he did not want to do the emotional work. Like many men, he was at his best giving within the traditional boundaries of male and female sex roles, adding some changes reflecting the impact of feminism and New Age masculinity (that is, sharing household chores, child care). I do not want to give the impression that I was emotionally together and therefore superior to him; I had my spaces of emotional lack. However, I had done a lot more work, both therapeutic and otherwise, around the issue of love.

At the time that I was experiencing my most intense longing to leave this relationship, Robin Norwood's 1985 book, *Women Who Love Too Much*, was published. It rocked the world. The feminist movement had launched a devastating critique at conventional ways of thinking about heterosexual love and romance, but it had not encouraged the development of new theories and publication of numerous books on the subject of love—books that would have illuminated for us how to make abiding, joyous relationships in the context of patriarchal culture. Stepping into the gap, the place where masses of women, irrespective of our sexual preferences, were registering unhappiness with love, self-help books (most of which were nonfeminist) offered direction and guidance. Ironically, the feminist movement had created a powerful audience for the self-help literature that made little or no mention of women's liberation. When it was mentioned, it was most often in a negative context.

On one hand, Norwood's book appropriated and echoed the feminist critique that women were too concerned about love and, on the other hand, in a decidedly antifeminist manner, it then "blamed" women for our failure to find fulfilling love. There was no discussion of patriarchy or male domination in Norwood's book. Men were not held accountable for failing to embrace emotional growth. She did not discuss the extent to which male with-holding and other forms of psychological terrorism culti-vated in women the desire to please and placate. There was no critique of male domination, no critical comment about patriarchy.

Positively, she provided women new ways to describe problems. Terms like "codependency" and "enabling" were useful to the extent that they offered ways for women to understand and talk about the no-win behavior of try-ing to elicit emotional response and feeling from partners who were emotionally closed and choosing to remain emotionally unavailable. However, Norwood's betrayal of women was marked by her demand that females assume all responsibility for correcting the problem.

Essentially, Norwood revised the old script. Like the tra-ditional gender narrative that had given women the role of creating love, demanding that we become sacrificial nur-turers and caregivers, always placing the good of others above our own good, the new narrative still made the task of creating love woman's work. Yet it simultaneously admonished women to stop being emotionally needy, so that we would not have to worry about whether we were being shortchanged. Basically, Norwood, like unenlight-ened feminist activists, encouraged women to imitate the behavior of their male counterparts—to repress and deny longings for love and simply come up with useful strate-gies (even though they might occasionally be manipulative ones) for getting needs met. The strategy Norwood offered that I applied in my relationship, which had increasingly become a site of endless conflicts—some of which culminated in abusive behavior—was to respond by saying the word "oh." For example: If your husband or partner did not return home at the time he stated he would, or at a reasonable hour, rather than complaining or saying anything to him about his behavior, the word "oh" should be stated. Uttering this single word would potentially defuse a volatile situation.

Now, I used this strategy many times. It worked. My partner at the time was quite pleased when, instead of discussing inappropriate behavior or making any verbal demand that he assume responsibility for his actions, I simply uttered the word "oh." As anyone who has worked in the field of domestic violence or been its target knows, conflict (whether verbal or physical abuse) often occurs when a woman initiates discussion. On many occasions, passive response could keep such conflict from happening. However, even though many of us used the word "oh" to effectively keep the peace and change the mood in our households, lots of women were slapped or hit for uttering this word. Of course, Norwood's response to those women who had been or were being abused was that they should leave. Yet in her book she never set forth any realistic guidelines for how women without economic self-sufficiency would just use some of that "love too much" energy to walk away.

Despite its flaws, its basic antifeminism, lots of women felt that *Women Who Love Too Much* helped them stop enabling codependent behavior. Unfortunately, it also silenced women's concerns about love. Since it offered no progressive insights for how women who wanted intimacy, especially relationships with men, might forge loving bonds within a patriarchal context, it did not intervene on the existing problem. Certainly, it in no way encouraged men to think about their role in the art of loving. In the wake of Norwood's book, its overwhelming popular reception, it became taboo for women to act publicly as though love mattered (since everyone was afraid of being identified as a woman who loved too much). In private, women continued to agonize about the question of love.

My women friends, who were almost all feminists, and I had spent years attending consciousness-raising groups and creating the space in intimate conversations to discuss and debate endlessly the nature of relationships and the meaning of love in the age of feminism. Those of us who remained emotionally and romantically involved with men were more obsessed than anyone with trying to create a blueprint for love that would provide guidelines for our daily lives. We wanted to know how to find, keep, and make love despite the power of the patriarchy. We wanted to strengthen our bonds with existing male partners. Concurrently, lesbian women in our circle were quick to call attention to the impact of patriarchal thinking on same-sex bonds. Many felt power struggles in their relationships were not that different from the struggles their heterosexual and bisexual peers were experiencing. As many lesbians as straight women were reading and praising the Norwood book.

I had entered my relationship at nineteen. And though we never married, I believed we would stay together "till death do us part." Leaving this relationship felt life-threatening, yet staying in it had also begun to feel life-threatening. I left when I entered midlife because I felt I had not yet known real love. And I did not want to end up like my mother, remaining in a relationship for my entire life wherein I felt deeply unloved. I was not alone.

Two years after the Norwood book, Shere Hite published her voluminous report *Women and Love*. Providing an accurate and realistic examination of women's attitudes toward love, her data suggested that far from loving "too much," most women were cynical about love. She reported that an overwhelming majority of women in relationships with men testified they did not feel loved. Hite commented, "Given the assumption in our society that one grows up, falls in love, and gets married, it's surprising that few women say that they are 'in love' with their husbands and how acceptable this seems to be to them." In her section "Loving Men at This Time in documented the reality that women involve that they had surrendered the hope of findii ing in its place the pleasures and/or benef companionship. In short, they began to do what Norwood had suggested—they gave up their desire for men to embrace emotional growth and become more loving. They repressed their own will to love. Denial and repression made life more bearable and relationships more satisfying.

By the end of the eighties, many women and men felt that the feminist movement had accomplished its most important goals. Terrific strides toward freedom and social equality with men had indeed happened. The world of labor outside the home was utterly changed. Women had become a major force in the work world, and there was no turning back to a time when most women had stayed home. Home life had been forever altered. While equality of domestic labor had not been achieved, most men contributed more to the upkeep and maintenance of households than in the past. Divorce had become completely acceptable, so that masses of women who were unhappy in marriages left or could leave them. Women initiated divorces more than men, oftentimes doing so not because of their desire to split but as a survival response to abusive and/or unkind male behavior. More and more women were coming out of the closet, testifying to the reality that lesbian relationships were as meaningful as other choices.

large group who had been heterosexual for most of their erotic lives were choosing to be involved exclusively with women. And as Hite documented, women over the age of forty, many of whom had spent all of their adult years in marriages or romantic bonds with men, reported finding a level of relational bliss never achieved in a heterosexual context. Lastly, more and more women, irrespective of their sexual leanings, were choosing to live alone.

In the wake of victories and triumphs, practically all feminist discussion of the meaning of love ceased. Hite had opened her book of revelations, *Women and Love,* with the declaration, "Women are suffering a lot of pain in their love relationships with men." A few pages later, in the introduction, she wrote, "I have always felt that 'love,' perhaps because it is considered to be the center, if not the totality of a woman's life, is a risky business, and one to which feminists should address much energy and ingenuity." This was and is such a powerful insight. Prophetically, Hite understood the necessity of creating a body of work on love by feminist thinkers, male and female, that would offer new insights as well as concrete testimony. That body of literature has not been produced.

Our sustained longing for love has not been fully addressed, for fear that to name it would somehow undermine an image of powerful, self-actualized feminist womanhood. Without a sustained, inspired vision of mutual love, our culture revises again and again old stories. Denial is never the setting for lasting empowerment. Tragically, our silence about love strengthens the backlash. By the beginning of the nineties, the mantra "What's love got to do with it?" had become the accepted theme. A passion for love had to be kept secret—unstated. To speak one's longing was to risk shame. Those who knew love enjoyed its delights in private, and those who did not know love suffered in silence. No feminist woman proclaimed loudly that she was looking for love. All of us were encouraged to act as though the workforce, careers, and money were more important than love. There was no space for women to speak our disappointment. We could not say that work was failing to provide us a space of fulfillment or that we were unfulfilled in our private, intimate lives. We were afraid to talk about the absence of love. Publicly, most women acted as though power was more important than love. This untruth had to be unmasked for us to place love on the agenda again—and insist that there has to be a balance between work and love.

gaining power, losing love

EMINIST women stopped talking about love because we found that love was harder to get than power. Men, and patriarchal females, were more willing to give us jobs, power, or money than they were to give us love. And many of us wanted and needed money. Bombarded by statistics that talked about how a woman's income dropped to next to nothing when she left a marriage with a man, I wanted to be clear about my economic fate before I left my long-time companion. He was both older than I and more established. Traditional sexist romantic myths had always made the older, more established male seem more desirable. Feminism had taken those myths and showed us all the ways they did not benefit women. We had been shown how an older, more established male, even the most benevolent of patriarchs, invariably exercised power over the less established, less powerful female. For example: Feminism encouraged women not to be the nurse hoping to marry the doctor but to become the doctor. And, then, if you wanted to marry another doctor—fine. Then the power would be equal.

In my case, I was the undergraduate who was partners with an older graduate student. While he wrote his dissertation, I worked at the phone company. His income from fellowships and loans was still higher than mine. When I taught three classes without a doctoral degree, I made less than a third of what he made teaching three classes. He supported my desires to stay in graduate school, even though we both knew that I was not cut out for academic life. I did not play by other people's rules. All my life I had problems obeying patriarchal authority. Academia, like all other corporations in our nation, was and remains male-dominated. While my male partner was consistently encouraged by professors to believe he had a stellar future awaiting him in the academic world, I was told that I did not have "the proper demeanor."

Despite the differences in our academic circumstances, I wanted to be self-supporting. Like lots of women who had been tutored by feminism to take responsibility for our own lives, I believed wholeheartedly that it was my responsibility to pay my own way. Of course, uniting theory with practice was not easy. At one point I was working overtime to pay my equal share, and my partner truly felt sorry for me. I had to work so much harder than he did, and after I'd paid my share there was nothing left over. He, on the other hand, made so much more money that he could pay his equal share and still have disposable income. Throughout our relationship he always showed a willingness to offer economic support. He never felt I "had" to work. Most of my growing-up life, my mother had not worked, and I could see how much this intensified our father's control over her life. Frankly, I did not trust any man enough to be dependent on him economically. Still, it soon became clear that equality was not feasible given the difference in our earning powers.

After years of battling about money, we chose to organize our finances around the principle of equity rather than that of equality. "Equity" simply means "something that is fair or just." We looked at the amount of time we both spent earning wages, then looked at the difference in our incomes. The result was that he contributed two-thirds to our household account and I one-third. This money covered all our living expenses. His disposable income went into his account and my bit into mine. We had been living together for more than seven years before implementing this plan. And when we employed this model, all our arguments about money ceased.

Years later, when I was ready to leave this relationship, I planned my exit much as one might plan leaving a job. I was afraid and cautious because I had moved out for a brief period and encountered the first major difficulty— finding housing. Staying with feminist friends, in a matter of weeks I met a stream of women who had left longtime relationships just to be rid of conflict and unhappiness, only to find that they were unprepared for the reality of making it on their own. Many of these women had never really paid much attention to financial matters. Like sleep-walkers, they left relationships in a trance and awakened later to the realization that we live in a material universe where money matters. These women were bitter. Some of them had been single for years, yet they were still full of rage and hostility toward ex-partners. Many of them had been screwed by "no fault" divorces, which feminists supported, realizing late in the game that women in longtime marriages who had been out of the workforce would suffer economically. Not only did they feel that their hearts had been broken, but also they felt they were still paying the price for wanting out. They were destitute. They worked long hours but barely earned enough money to make ends meet. They had trouble finding housing. The list of their complaints was long. And they were all eager to affirm that "patriarchy rules." Listening to them, I realized that I was neither financially nor emotionally ready to be single.

I returned home realizing that the best action I could take in the direction of my independence was to finish my dissertation and look for a job. Ironically, during this period the relationship was harmonious. Yet when I finished and the job search began, life became more complicated. When I was finally offered a job at a prestigious Ivy League institution far away from our home, the debates began. My partner was not certain that he wanted to request a year's leave without pay and come live with me. Previously, I had followed him to every job in any city he chose to take. When he showed hesitation as my turn came, I felt betrayed. This time, I decided, I was really leaving.

Recovering emotionally from the loss of this relationship took years longer than had my efforts to become completely economically self-sufficient. However, if I had not attended to material matters in a practical manner, I might never have recovered. To this day I might be mired in the bitterness and rage that many women are stuck in when they leave, in midlife, relationships that have lasted for more than ten years. Many men use material privilege as a weapon against women when they want to end relationships. The longer the relationship, the more intense the conflict over shared material resources. I was lucky. My partner and I were equitable and just in our distribution of resources. Even when there were minor conflicts, they were resolved.

Women faced with the requirement that they be fully economically independent, some for the first time in midlife, were necessarily more concerned about finances than they were about love. Significantly, however, it was easier for women to address economic concerns than it was for them to address the issue of love. We did not have a language to talk about the reality that love did not prevail in our relationships with men. Among us feminists, the men we had loved were individuals who claimed to care about injustice. Many of these males had put their lives on the line when it came to battling with issues of race or class exploitation and oppression. Verbally, they had championed our struggle for women's rights. However, when we began to talk feminist revolution, wanting far more than equal rights, when we began to demand an entire cultural transformation, one that would require that the terms of masculinity be altered and reconstructed, more often than not the men in our lives did not wholeheartedly stand by us. For many of us, this failure of solidarity was most graphically and painfully registered in our intimate lives. Our male comrades' refusal to change their thinking about sexuality, especially sexist conditioning socializing them to believe that women existed to satisfy their desire on demand, made it clear that they were not willing to give up all the privileges accorded them by patriarchy. Their refusal to adequately confront the ways sexist socialization had denied them access to emotional and spiritual growth was yet another arena of betrayal.

Our heartache came from facing the reality that if men were not willing to holistically embrace feminist revolution, then they would not be in an emotional place where they could offer us love. There can be no love without justice. If, at the end of the day, progressive men were unwilling to be just in their relationships with women on all fronts, public and private, then what they were communicating to us was a lack of genuine political solidarity. Only individual lesbian separatists active in feminist movement had the courage to loudly call out this betrayal. However, their critique of men was most often dismissed as mere sexual rivalry and seduction (that is, they wanted all the women for themselves) or depicted as yet another example of man hating.

Brokenhearted heterosexual feminists did not want to testify publicly that men would support equal rights for women in every arena but the sexual. To offer this testimony would have necessitated admitting that male conversion to feminist thinking and practice was needed if we were truly to have a successful feminist revolution. And women were not eager to acknowledge publicly the ways feminism had failed to convert men to feminist thinking and practice. Complete feminist culture transformation could happen without male allies only if women were willing to sacrifice their desire to have primary relationships with men. If that had been the case, male withholding of regard, recognition, and reciprocity in the sexual arena would not have mattered.

Emotionally overwhelmed by the reality of straight

men's attachment to holding power over women in the sexual arena, feminist women just wanted to turn the channel. We did not want to examine why it was we had not been able to fully convert men to feminist thinking and practice. We did not want to acknowledge out loud that feminist demands had been compromised, that many of us were settling for equality and power in the public arena while continuing to conform to sexist gender roles at home or, most important, in the bedroom. Let me reiterate here that many men who were willing to be househusbands, to take care of the kids, to be advocates for equal pay for equal work, to do their share or even all of the housekeeping, were not willing to change in any way their sexual habits.

Indeed, the intersection of women's liberation and sexual liberation actually made feminism more appealing to men. The invention and mass production of the birth-control pill may have freed women's sexual bodies, but it was feminism that freed our minds. Feminist demand for sexual agency made us feel that we were engaged in revolutionary struggle when we boldly satisfied our sexual lust. We had been given permission to give blow jobs if we wanted to, but only if we wanted to. We had been given the freedom to be sexually loose without fear of losing respect. And lots of straight men were more than enthralled with a movement that freed all women from the prison of sexual fear and/or frigidity.

Contrary to the sexual myths about "smart" girls projected by the male patriarchal pornographic imagination, independent women were more fun to be sexual with. Straight men were thrilled to encounter sexually liberated feminist females who also paid their share of the date. Conflicts and problems began when the wanton feminist cared to exercise complete control over her body and say no when she wanted to. Feminists' refusal to make satisfying male desire the primary goal of female sexual liberation disturbed men. When we fully exercised our right to say no, then men who were our allies in struggle in other ways were suddenly afraid of losing their open and easy access to sexual fulfillment. For example: There is not one essay written by a feminist man who likes having his dick sucked that tells us how he copes with having a longtime female partner who refuses to perform fellatio. Maybe she refuses because the adult man who abused her as a child forced her to put his penis in her mouth. Maybe she refused because the teenage boy with whom she first had oral sex violently pushed her head down on his dick and would not allow her to catch her breath, so she felt as though she were being strangled. A number of scenarios could possibly explain her distaste for fellatio, but how does her feminist male partner affirm her reality while coping with the fact that she will not satisfy his desire?

Conversely, extremely powerful feminist women in longtime marriages and partnerships with less powerful men who refuse to be sexual with them do not write essays on the subject. In private conversations with other women from time to time, they may acknowledge the ways this male sexual withholding mediates female power as it renders them needy and emotionally vulnerable, but in general they do not promote public discourse about this topic. Most heterosexual women will testify that the men in our lives are more willing to engage in communicative, reciprocal, caring behavior outside the bedroom when they feel satisfied inside it. Few feminist women have had the courage to talk about the extent to which achieving power and success may have made them fearful of losing male partners and therefore more willing to engage privately in erotic acts that subordinate females to males. What if the real discovery that feminists could not speak was the fact that men did not care if we were their equals everywhere, including the battlefield, as long they remained our superiors—the ones in charge, the ones on top—in the bedroom? And nobody, but nobody, ever talks about the men married to more powerful economically self-sufficient women who upset these gains in equal rights by denying her sexual attentions. What if straight women active in the feminist movement had been simply too homophobic to admit that lesbian women who had questioned our continued erotic allegiance to men were right to question whether we asserted equal rights when it came to sexual performance?

Maybe it has been easier for women to talk publicly

about sexual sadomasochism when they find it difficult or even taboo to talk about love because men find one topic sexy and the other one trite. In the nineties we had little insightful feminist discourse on love, while we had all manner of public talk about sexual sadomasochism. Self-proclaimed feminist thinkers have colluded with the patriarchal pornographic imagination's use of mass media to represent the sexual resubordination of women by men as cute, playful, and harmless. While many of the rights women gained as a consequence of feminist struggle are being taken from us (reproductive rights; the right to challenge sexual violence at home, on the streets, and in the workplace; the right to earn equal pay for equal work, which has never been successfully institutionalized in all work arenas), we are bombarded with images suggesting that male sexual domination of women in no way threatens female autonomy or independence. In actuality, male domination of females in the sexual arena (whether they maintain control by wanting too much sex or none at all) is a constant reminder that females are not free, that we have not attained full equal rights or equity.

All the women who gained more power and money as a result of the feminist movement who now choose to disassociate themselves from its politics do so in part to win favor with men. The vast majority of men have shown us for some time now that they do not find feminism sexy. While it may give them a thrill to encounter an independent female, that thrill lasts only if they undermine and subordinate her power. Sex gets more attention than love from feminist women and everyone else because when we speak of love we have to speak of loss, of lack, of our failures of will and courage. It is not easy to face that men, even politically progressive men, may want sexual power over women more than they want to love us. Highlighting her own desperation to be loved by the most important male in her life in the memoir *Daddy, We Hardly Knew You,* Germaine Greer argues that women have a stake in pretending that patriarchal men really care about female well-being. Boldly, she states, "Women are always ready to believe that men love them, despite all appearances to the contrary." Able to surrender and share public power with women, many men are unable to offer the emotional surrender needed to give love.

If feminists had continued to talk about love, then we would have needed to speak about the extreme lovelessness that is at the heart of domination. We would not have been able to go forward with our newly acquired equal rights, jobs, money, and power without telling everyone that we had discovered that patriarchy, like any colonizing system, does not create the context for women and men to love one another. We would have needed to remind everyone repeatedly that genuine love between females and males could emerge only in a context where the sexes would come together to challenge and change patriarchal thought. To continue to speak of love, we would have had to break through the wall of denial that seduces us all to accept subordination and domination as natural facts of everyday life. We would be telling everyone, especially the men in our lives, again and again that domination and love do not go together, that if one is present, the other is not. We would not have allowed our fathers, brothers, male comrades, or lovers to continue to believe they love us when they hurt us again and again. Men do not wound women only when they act violently and abusively. They wound us when they fail to protect our freedom in every aspect of our daily lives.

Females coming to womanhood in the wake of contemporary feminist movement are among that group who are the most cynical about love and the most fascinated by power. Among these late-twenties and thirty-something groups are women who are coming to power by acquiring unprecedented wealth and fame. These women know that it is easier for them to acquire material resources than to find love. In the epilogue to *Bitch,* Elizabeth Wurtzel laments, "None of us are getting better at love: we are getting more scared of it. We were not given good skills to begin with, and the choices we make have tended only to reinforce our sense that it is hopeless and useless." We are indeed living in an age when women and men are more likely to long for power than they are to long for love. We can all speak of our longing for power. Our longing for love must be kept secret. To give voice to such longing is to be counted among the weak, the soft.

No wonder, then, that women who yearn to know love often feel they have no choice but to return to conventional ways of thinking about coupling and romance. Even though those ways fail, they at least hold out the promise and possibility of fulfillment. Right now we are fast becoming a nation where no one values love, one where women eschew the politics of love for the politics of power.

Ongoing male violence against females daily stands as public testimony to the failure of feminist movement to convert and change the hearts of men. Ironically, we now live in a culture in which male verbal harassment of an individual woman on the job can become a global topic, discussed night after night on television everywhere, yet we cannot draw ongoing, serious attention to the everyday forms of violence against women in the home, because to do so would disrupt the love story that tells us men and women will live happily ever after. Feminist silence about love reflects a collective sorrow about our powerlessness to free all men from the hold patriarchy has on their minds and hearts. It reflects our shock at male betrayal. It has not been that difficult to show women the ways in which their continued allegiance to patriarchal thinking hurts them and other women. It has been hard to inspire them to give up that allegiance when it provides them common ground on which to meet and bond with men.

Women and men who are still seduced by domination cannot know love. Yet everywhere we turn, our culture tells us we can still know love even in the midst of relationships charged with coercive pain and domination. The time has come to tell the truth. Again. There is no love without justice. Men and women who cannot be just deny themselves and everyone they choose to be intimate with the freedom to know mutual love. If we remain unable to imagine a world where love can be recognized as a unifying principle that can lead us to seek and use power wisely, then we will remain wedded to a culture of domination that requires us to choose power over love. Women have searched for power and found it.

Nowadays most women and men acknowledge the rightness of gender equality. We have created a culture in which women can be the equals of patriarchal men, where power in all its forms is shared among the sexes, however inequitably. But we have not created a culture of gender equality that encourages women and men to search for love with the same zeal and passion that inspires our quest for success and power. Until that world comes into being, women may gain greater and greater power yet find themselves equal participants in promoting a culture of lovelessness, where everyone loses and love cannot be found.

women who fail at loving

WOMEN are not inherently more interested in or more able to love than are men. From girlhood on, we learn to be more enchanted with love. Since the business of loving came to be identified as woman's work, females have risen to the occasion and claimed love as our topic. Females sit with one another every day and talk about love. The most popular movies and television shows with women as the lead characters are all about the female search for love. We begin our conversations about love in girlhood and are still talking about love as elderly women approaching death. Our obsession with love is sanctioned and sustained by the culture we live in.

Love came fully into the picture for women only in the nineteenth century, when marriage came to be seen as more than a bonding whose primary purpose was the sharing of resources and the breeding of future workers. European imperialist colonization of other cultures made it possible to idealize female submission. The growth of capitalism allowed there to be a split between home and work, the private and the public. Women's task in the private domain was to create a harmonious household. In the public domain, men could be competitive and unkind. Home was the place where these passions could be tamed. There a man could sit back and relax, as it was woman's task to create a peaceful, nurturing universe. This image of home led to the idealization of motherhood.

As mothers, women were supposed to be innately concerned with sustaining life—with nurturance. As protectors and providers, men could take life (as they did in imperialistic wars) or they could be ruthless in the workplace. Departing from the classical Greek and Roman ideal that had made love the primary province of men relating to men, as love could exist only between equals, from the focus on God as an all-loving parent, or notions of romantic mutual love, new love stories assigned love to the sphere of domesticity. In her book *A Natural History of Love,* Diane Ackerman describes this shift: "Women were to stay at home and tend the children; men returned home after work and spent time with them and the children. All the important decisions affecting the family were made by the man, the lord of the manor, whose home, modest though it might have been, was his castle. When romantic love sifted through the new dreams of the middle class, it became domesticated, simplified, tidy, sexless."

Women's economic dependence on men was to have been mediated by male emotional dependency on women. Perhaps no one foresaw that individual male misogynists, believing in the natural superiority of men, would continue to rigorously construct a counternarrative, one in which to be emotional was to be inferior. Rather than men's collectively delighting in their emotional dependency on women, they began to devalue the realm of emotions, which meant, of course, that they devalued love.

In the patriarchal male imagination, the subject of love was relegated to the realm of the weak and replaced by narratives of power and domination. For men, satisfying sexual desire became more important than the art of loving. Sex could take precedence over love because it was like work, a domain where one could engage in power plays. Unlike the desire for mutual love, which could happen only with effortful engagement, sexual passion could be easily fulfilled. As men turned away from love, the meaning of love was obscured. Ideas about love that emphasized a soul mate, reciprocal care and devotion, were supplanted by an emphasis on sacrificial care and nurturance. Love became solely woman's work.

Women, idealized as mothers, were seen as uniquely situated for the task of nurturance. The working man of the twentieth century had no time for realizing a love rooted in romantic traditions, which required of the love devotion and communication. His time was not his own. It was the duty of the wife/mother to produce this love by herself in the factory of the home and offer it to the man when he returned. Debates about whether females are "natural" nurturers and therefore more suited to the practice of love than their male counterparts have consistently occurred in feminist circles. Psychologists like Jean Baker Miller and Carol Gilligan have claimed that there are major sex differences, based on women's greater capacity for caring and relational connection. In their insightful study, *Singing at the Top of Our Lungs: Women, Love, and Creativity,* Claudia Bepko and Jo-Ann Krestan critique this standpoint: "While Gilligan's and Miller's work marked a shift away from the prevailing theories that viewed female experience only in terms of male development and found it inherently inferior, they nevertheless supported certain ways of thinking that tend to reinforce the notion that men and women are 'essentially' different rather than having different experiences based on the ways that split images make them think about themselves. In their view, men are defined by the need for autonomy and women by the need for attachment. Yet we know that men crave intimacy as much as women and women crave autonomy as much as men. Issues of relationship and connection versus autonomy and differentiation are more culturally determined."

Rather than being inherently able to nurture, females learn how to nurture or how to pretend that they are nurturing.

Girls learn how to be "mothers" by imitating female caretakers and by ritual play with dolls. Male children are not consistently taught how to nurture. Instead they are most often aggressively socialized to reject nurturance and choose domination. War games and all games of pretend violence teach boys that their role is to take life when necessary. Most boys learn that to be truly masculine they must be able to take life, not to give and nurture life. Even though individual men can participate more in parenting because feminism called attention to the importance and value of male nurturance, men overall do not want to parent. In her book on parenting, *The Mother Dance*, Harriet Lerner emphasizes that "when nurturing children is truly valued, mothers who work at home will be economically protected and men will want to join us as equal partners in parenting. As it is now, men who wax sentimental about motherhood are rarely scurrying about trying to make career trade-offs in order to be home more with their young children." No one believes that males are inherently capable of nurturance, but this sexist stereotype continues to shape cultural perceptions about female identity.

Of course, we need only examine the incredible statistics of child abuse inflicted by females to see hard evidence that women are not naturally more prone to give nurturance and care. Even women who believe the sexist thinking that they are biologically destined to be caregivers act out violently in their role as parents. The lived experience of women who mother offers the greatest challenge to theories suggesting that women are the kinder, gentler, more caring, more ethically moral sex. Despite all the evidence to the contrary, patriarchal men, along with men who claim to be feminist allies, appropriated Gilligan's positive emphasis on differences between the sexes. John Gray's phenomenal bestseller *Men Are from Mars, Women Are from Venus: A Practical Guide for Improving Communication and Getting What You Want in Your Relationships,* exploits the trend to attach value to women's supposedly different ways of knowing. While appearing to be an advocate of equality between the sexes, in all his work John Gray reinscribes and overvalues the very stereotypes about sexual difference that feminist scholarship by women and men has worked so hard to disprove.

Like Gilligan, Gray evokes again and again an image of women that suggests we are innately more inclined toward relational connection than men are. Unlike her, he does not employ this thesis to suggest it would enhance male self-development to be more relational; instead he privileges male emotional withdrawal. Basically, Gray approaches problems in male-female relationships as if patriarchy did not exist and as if male domination were not a reality. In the relational universe he evokes, conflict or unhappiness among heterosexuals is most often just the outcome of miscommunication. In his book on parenting, *Children Are from Heaven,* Gray reminds readers in a section on "gender differences" that "from day one, boys will be boys and girls will be girls." Sexist thinking about the nature of male and female roles is reinforced in this work.

In Gray's work, male lack of interest in emotional connection is always treated as though it were normal and natural. Yet he most reveals his underlying support of patriarchy by the way in which he makes a virtue of male withholding. The fact that men use emotional withholding as a weapon of psychological terrorism is never discussed. It is a woman's fault if she lacks the skills to cope with male withholding. Gray comes to the rescue by offering guidelines for how she can acquire those skills. For example: He tells women if they do not want to be hurt by a withholding man who retreats into a cave, they should not disturb him by seeking connection. His books are useful to the extent that they offer women strategies for how to live harmoniously with sexist men.

When I rushed out to buy a copy of *Men Are from Mars, Women Are from Venus,* I did so because I welcome any new insights that may lead to better understanding between women and men. Ironically, when I read the book, I found his characterizations of women and what we were like so far removed from real life that I thought they were ridiculously funny. Yet when I got to the section on men, the behavior described did indeed correspond to that of sexist males I encounter on the streets, at work, and in relationships. His strategies for better communication between the sexes often work, but they do not challenge or change sexism. Tragically, his work does not invite women and men to see the extent to which patriarchal thinking creates the very differences in behavior between women and men that he valorizes.

Gray not only romanticizes and covers up male sexism, he colludes with conventional thinking in offering a portrait of women that suggests that we are innately more interested in caregiving and nurturance. Women are not violent and abusive toward children in Gray's universe. Relationships between adults and children are not talked about by him in ways that expose the reality of power dynamics between female parents and children over whom they exercise autocratic control. To do so would certainly challenge the one-dimensional construction of females as inherently nurturing or desirous of connection that he evokes.

Almost all liberal New Age men writing about relationships embrace the notion of "essential" masculine and feminine qualities. In addition, they may raise the idea of androgyny, suggesting that every man and woman has these qualities, that given their respective gender it is important that they keep the balance of power on the correct side (that is, a man does not want to nurture his feminine qualities so that they overshadow his masculine ones). In the book *Mars and Venus Together Forever*, Gray cautions, "If a very masculine man becomes more feminine, he is moving toward balance. But if he is already too much on his female side, pushing him farther into it creates greater imbalance." The relational universe evoked in books by New Age men, with the exception of John Bradshaw's work, is rarely one where the power of patriarchy is named or its ideology spelled out. The insistence that there is a naturally biologically based world of sex differences is at the heart of patriarchal thinking. Liberal women and men cannot embrace this thinking and perpetuate it without maintaining an allegiance to patriarchy.

Antipatriarchal thinking acknowledges the reality of biological differences between genders but recognizes that cultural conditioning has shown itself to be stronger than anatomy—and that anatomy is not destiny. Most feminist thinkers would agree that an individual female is more likely to be socialized to be a nurturer than is her male counterpart. That socialization may neatly correspond to the biological reality that a child in the womb is nurtured by the body of the mother. Yet there is much hard evidence that documents the reality that women who have passively nurtured a child in the womb may be completely indifferent to the needs of a newborn infant. A vast majority of females giving birth for the first time do not have a clue about what they should do. Conscientious expectant mothers try to learn what they need to do to care for newborns before the child is born.

Until our culture can break through myth and accept that women are not innately capable of nurturing others, the assumption that women are better able to love than men will prevail. Sexist women are as likely as their male counterparts, if not more so, to insist that women are naturally better caregivers. In actuality, nurturance—the ability to care for another in a manner that enhances well-being— is a learned behavior. Men learn it as well as women. Patriarchal culture is reinforced when males are not taught ways to nurture and care for others. One of the most useful insights of contemporary feminist thought, which should be common sense by now, is the recognition that adult males who are parented in a healthy manner learned through that process how to be nurturers. Males who take primary care of infants from birth forward are as bonded with the children they nurture as females.

To a grave extent, some women have enjoyed one-upping men in the emotional caregiving arena, even though so many women are wounded by male inability to give care. These women steadfastly cling to sexist stereotypes that depict women as innately better caregivers than men. Their collusion with patriarchal culture makes it harder for males of all ages to gain access to the skills that would allow them to be better nurturers. This adds to the gender crisis. When men are able to assume an equal role with women as caregivers, it becomes most evident that they can nurture as well as women.

An overemphasis on female capacity for caregiving has led many people to make nurturing synonymous with love. In fact, the ability to nurture, to give care, is only one aspect of love. Psychoanalyst Erich Fromm's groundbreaking book *The Art of Loving* defined love as an action informed by care, respect, knowledge, and responsibility. Care alone does not create love. Time and time again, individuals testify that women, especially those who are not fully self-actualized, who are given only the task of nurturing others, can use nurturance as a way to render the recipients of their care unduly dependent. Some individual women nurture in ways that are so overbearing and invasive of the boundaries of the folks they care for that they do more to alienate and/or violate than to enhance growth. The concept of codependence emerged from the awareness of this danger.

Conditioned to hone nurturing skills while failing to cultivate agency in all other ways, women are likely to be no more able to learn the art of loving than are their male counterparts. Certainly an individual who knows how to be a caregiver is one step ahead of another individual who has no idea how to give care when it comes to the art of loving. When I read John Gray's books and he is teaching men, or telling women how to teach men, to make basic conversation by asking questions like "How was your day?" or "How are you feeling?" I can be easily convinced that females from Venus are more emotionally together than are males from Mars. However, I would rather inhabit an earthly paradise where males and females learn how to communicate care for others when we are children.

Significantly, many female nurturers have raised boy children single-handedly (or with little input from fathers, be they present or absent) who lack these skills. Harriet Lerner stresses again and again in her work on parenting that "the notion of 'maternal instinct' as a universal driving force for all women is a fantasy." And that fantasy has provided the more powerful cover-up for female failure to give care to children. When mothers know how to give care, how to nurture, they can impart these skills to girls and boys. My brother was the only boy in a household of six sisters. He was taught how to communicate and give care when he was a young child, learning the same lessons his sisters learned. However, when he entered adolescence, he learned from the world outside the home, from male peers, that it was more masculine to behave in an uncaring manner toward others. For a short time he went into the withholding, disrespectful-of-others mode, particularly of females, and he ceased communicating. Using John Gray's books, we could say "he entered his cave."

Our mother tolerated this behavior for a brief period.

But I can still remember the day he came home from junior high after basketball practice and bounded through the living room past his mom and sisters, not saying a word. He was rushing to change to play with waiting friends. Mom waited until he reached his room, and just as he was about to rush out, she stopped him and explained the manner in which his actions were uncaring and disrespectful. She requested that he rewind the tape, go out again, come in again, and acknowledge with respect and/or care—depending on his feelings—the presence of his mother and sisters, the bond he shared with us. Socialized in his growing-up years to communicate and give care, my brother knows how to nurture. Just as he knows that in patriarchal culture, nurturing men are not as respected as men who withhold care.

Even though women usually know more about caregiving than men do because we have been taught these skills from girlhood on, we do not instinctively or innately know how to give love. Care is an aspect of love, but it is not the same. It fascinates me that females are usually more socialized than males to speak of our longing for love, even to crave love, when there is no connection made between the cultivation of these feelings and the fact that we are not taught how to give and receive love. The same patriarchal conditioning that teaches females to believe we are innately nurturing teaches us that we will instinctively know how to give and receive love. We fail at love as much as men do because we simply do not know what we are doing.

Women are often more interested in being loved than in the act of loving. All too often the female search for love is epitomized by this desire, not by a desire to know how to love. Until we are able to acknowledge that women fail at loving because we are no more schooled in the art of loving than are our male counterparts, we will not find love. If the female obsession with love in patriarchal culture were linked from birth on to the practice of love, then women would be experts in the art of loving. And as a consequence, since women do most of the parenting in our nation, children would be more loving. If women excelled in the art of loving, these skills would be imparted to male and female children alike.

As long as our culture devalues love, women will remain no more able to love than our male counterparts are. In patriarchal culture, giving care continues to be seen as primarily a female task. The feminist movement did not change this perception. And while women more than men are often great caregivers, this does not translate into knowing how to be loving. Love is a combination of care, commitment, knowledge, responsibility, respect, and trust. Socialized in the art of caring, it is easier for women who desire to love to learn the necessary skills to practice love. And yet women have not chosen to give themselves wholeheartedly over to the art of loving. As long as being loved is seen as a gesture of weakness, one that disempowers, women will remain afraid to love fully, deeply, completely. Women will continue to fail at love, because this failure places females on an equal footing with males who turn away from love. Women who fail at loving need not be disappointed that the men in their lives—fathers, siblings, friends, or lovers—do not give love. Women who learn to love represent the greatest threat to the patriarchal status quo. By failing to love, women make it clear that it is more vital to their existence to have the approval and support of men than it is to love.

choosing and learning to love

EFORE I reached the age of forty, I never even considered that my relationships did not last because I did not know enough about love. After all, I had lived with a male partner for fifteen years—and that seemed like a long time. When I left this relationship, I thought our failure to sustain meaningful intimacy was due to lacks in my partner and not in myself. Despite relentless scrutiny in a constructive manner of the problems we had encountered and failed to resolve, it never occurred to me to interrogate myself about whether I had been loving. I assumed that love was a given. Therein lay my mistake. My knowledge of love was not deep. All the philosophical ways of thinking about love in my life had come from books. Translating theory into practice was much harder than simply reading about it. And like most women, I just assumed I was more loving than the man in my life.

After several years of living alone, I began to think seriously about my relationship to intimacy. Until then, I, like many women in similar circumstances, felt that the problems in my relationships were caused by my male partner's fear of intimacy. While I haven't had many partners, it was not hard to see similar threads running through the pattern of my relational choices. I chose men who were quiet, reserved, private, who were loners, often withholding and emotionally unavailable. They were all the adult children of alcoholics. They had all been raised by single mothers to whom they were very attached. In each case a quality I liked most in these relationships was the man's willingness to accept my autonomy. When I left my longest relationship, I would often joke that we had been better at giving each other space to be separate selves than we had been at creating and sustaining the spaces of togetherness.

Being alone and celibate gave me the psychic space to confront myself and examine my relationship to intimacy. Soon it was obvious that I had chosen partners who were not particularly "into" intimacy, because then I had never had to make a leap of faith, to trust, or to risk. Being with men who were not interested in offering abiding closeness meant that I never really had to be close. Yet I could have an image of myself as this open, giving woman who really desired closeness, at times feeling smug because I worked so hard on the "relationship." Working to be close with someone who is not interested in sustained closeness not only depresses the spirit, it makes you a perfect target for aggression. As John Gray endlessly tells us in *Men Are from Mars, Women Are from Venus,* when withholding men do not want to be close, watch out, because they are likely to attack if you reach out to them seeking intimate interaction.

Many women who are warm and openhearted choose men who are closed and shut down because we hope we can provide a catalyst for them to open up. Our efforts usually fail, because these men have not made their own commitment to being more open. Trained to be nurturers and caregivers, women often think we are behaving as we should—doing what we have been socialized to believe is a woman's job. We may even experience the constant tension between these two different value systems—a man who has chosen to avoid intimacy and a woman who desires intimacy—as stimulating. Importantly, though, this unfulfilling work keeps us from the real work of intimacy.

Alone with myself, I chose to look closely at my relationship to intimacy. I found that I, like many creative women seeking to be successful in a career or vocation, was actually deeply afraid of bonding with a man who would make the kind of demands for closeness that might be all-consuming. I had grown up in a patriarchal household where my mother had waited on my father hand and foot. When she was not meeting his needs, she was meeting the needs of her children. Her needs were rarely, if ever, met. I am not even sure that she could have articulated her needs and desires, because she had been so well trained to believe that a good wife and mother has no desires beyond the welfare of her family. Most of the marriages and relationships I saw were ones in which women were always the primary caregivers and had little time for self-development.

Talking about her own life, Jane Jervis, the president of Evergreen State College, in the speech "Composing a Life. You Can Have It All but Not All at Once," describes growing up with a mother who encouraged her children to seek higher education, who set an example by getting a degree in biochemistry in midlife. Initially Jane refused to follow in her mother's footsteps, choosing to be the married woman behind the man. She said, "I remember being thirty-something and rummaging in the kitchen cabinets of my life . . . and feeling that nothing in there was mine—every single thing in the cabinets of my life was for somebody else. Holly liked celery, no onions, in her tuna fish; Cindy liked onions, no celery; Ken liked onions and celery—so I always made three batches of tuna fish and suddenly realized that I didn't even know how I liked it myself." Significantly, her development was waylaid when she fell in love her freshman year in college. But the problem was not that she fell in love but that she fell into a relationship/marriage wherein their mutual growth and development was not their primary agenda. There are still too few models of heterosexual relationships in which mutual growth is the foundational bonding principle. I had no models of mutual love when I entered college.

Studying the lives of women writers whose work I admired, I looked to these literary mentors to guide me in my search for love. A devotee of Sylvia Plath's poetry, I can still remember weeping once as I read somewhere that she would rise early in the morning to sit and write her poems before her children awakened. Just on the verge of adult womanhood, I wept knowing that she had not survived the effort to balance the multiple longings and desires that ruled her life, the desires to be a writer, a wife, a mother. With no role models, I was uncertain about the path to take. I wanted to be a writer, but I also wanted a meaning-ful relationship. Afraid of being engulfed and consumed by relationships, distracted from developing my artistic and intellectual abilities, I was drawn toward men who were supportive of these endeavors and who were not emotionally demanding. Too late I realized that their lack of emotional demands was linked to a lack of interest in emotional openness or personal growth. Perhaps they, too, were afraid of engulfment, only in their case having been raised by demanding, overprotective single mothers, maybe they feared a female's exercising too much control over their choices and actions.

When we choose partners who enable us to grow in ways that are important to us, it is all the more difficult to see destructive behavior patterns when they arise. Since most of us have been raised to think care is the primary, if not the sole, ingredient of love, we are easily able to convince ourselves that we are "in love." So many women have never been nurtured in any way by a male, and as a consequence it can be quite enthralling to receive care, especially from a male partner. Each one of my partners supported my intellectual and creative work in ways that I still appreciate and value, whereas the lack of mature emotional interaction helped retard my emotional growth.

Positioned to be primary caregivers, women are often arrogant when it comes to matters of the heart. Believing the mystification of our sexist social conditioning, which encourages us to assume we know how to love—as though desire and action were one and the same—we may suffer countless relational failures before we begin to think critically about the nature of love. Masses of women buy books, like those written by John Gray, Susan Jeffers, Barbara De Angelis, Pat Love, and other self-help gurus on the subject of love. We do so because we want to understand how to make heterosexual relationships work. The fact that these books sell millions of copies is no testament to their value; they are the primary vehicle for a practical discussion of intimate relationships that we have in our culture. Importantly, most of them offer strategies to help improve relationships without addressing the issue of love. Making a relationship "work" is not the same as "creating love."

One of the best books on the subject of love is John Bradshaw's *Creating Love: The Next Great Stage of Growth,* which was first published in 1992. Bradshaw, most known for his work on reclaiming the wounded inner child, deviates in this book from the usual self-help advice on love because he dares to courageously discuss the impact of patriarchal thinking on our ways of understanding love. This work did not have the incredible impact on contemporary culture that his previous work had. Readers bought it, but they were not willing to break through their denial about the ways in which patriarchy prevents us from knowing love. This book was challenging because it did not encourage women to see ourselves as more able to love than men. Nor did he pretend that male failure to love was somehow to be blamed on demanding women.

Bradshaw did not fall into the popular jargon about complementary sex differences that has become so much the norm in self-help works. Instead he insisted that women and men recognize the extent to which "even with the best intentions our parents often confused love with what we would now call abuse," giving us all a mystified understanding of what it means to love. Linking that abuse to cultural acceptance of patriarchal domination as a founding narrative, he illuminates our nation's elevation of narratives of power over love in our culture and in our families.

We all know that not everyone comes from an abusive family context, and we do know that almost all of us are raised in homes that value and uphold patriarchal thinking. When females are taught to believe we are more capable of giving love than are our male counterparts, we are embracing patriarchal assumptions. Those assumptions shape the way we think and act in intimate relationships. Women involved with men who believe that they are more able to love are predisposed to accept male emotional withholding. They already expect men to be deficient. This does not mean they do not hope that the male they are relating to will learn to be more emotionally giving; they do. The tragic irony here is that patriarchal thinking has socialized males to believe that their manhood is affirmed when they are emotionally withholding. Social conditioning creates the differences in the sexes we are encouraged to think are "natural" and simultaneously lays the groundwork for conflict.

Nothing indicts female allegiance to patriarchy more than the willingness to behave as though the problems created by cultural investment in sexist thinking about the nature of male and female roles can be solved by women's working harder. Women who cling to the notion that if they just simply change their behavior, then men will happily learn how to be more caring, are in denial. Their denial strengthens patriarchy, but it does not create a universe where women and men can love one another. Antipatriarchal thinking, which assumes that both women and men are equally capable of learning how to love, of giving and receiving love, is the only foundation on which to construct sustained, meaningful, mutual love.

Ultimately, women who desire to be loving and/or to make loving partnerships with men must be willing to unlearn sexist conditioning. And vice versa. Only when we approach love with a basic respect for men's emotional universe will we be able to recognize those men who are simply not ready to love and be loved. In her refreshingly feminist-based work *Life Preservers*, popular psychotherapist Harriet Lerner reminds us that "it's almost impossible to imagine what intimate relationships with men—or women—would look like in a different world of true gender equality." Because it is so difficult for women to conjure up a picture, it's all the more important that we start with a concrete understanding of what love is and the barriers to love already existing in our society.

There was a time when I arrogantly and naively thought that women were more loving than men. I thought this because we were the group I heard talking the most about love, seeking it, and celebrating it when we found it. We were also the group that talked the most about our disappointments in love. When it came to heterosexual love and romance, we were convinced men were the problem. The heady, fun years of contemporary feminism simply reinforced the idea that we women were superior to men when it came to our emotional universe. Then most women believed that we were better lovers because we had been trained to be caregivers—to nurture.

Even though a great many of us had been raised by tyrannical, codependent, immature women, many of whom were sometimes violent and abusive—usually via verbal shaming and humiliation—for the most part we were still clinging to the image of women as being "all heart." In my second book, *Feminist Theory: From Margin to Center,* first published in the early eighties, I included a chapter questioning the assumption that women are less violent than men, more caregiving, by calling attention to adult female child abuse. I pointed out that it is precisely the fact that many of our mothers are simultaneously abusive and caregiving that leads us to idealize them and to minimize the traumatic implications of their abusive behavior. Fathers who are primarily abusive, verbally or physically, rarely give sustained care and are rarely idealized. Sacrificial mother martyrs almost always give sustained care, even as they may also mix this care with dominating, coercive behavior. Indeed, more often than not it is maternal sadism that may be the early indoctrination that sets women up to confuse sadomasochistic intimate terrorism with love. Often the verbal shaming and humiliation that adult patriarchal men do to female partners mirror and reenact familiar forms of abuse females have experienced with dominating, punishing patriarchal mothers.

For many years I idealized and idolized my mother, seeing her as the victim of a sexist, patriarchal man. When I first consciously converted to feminist thinking, I idolized her all the more. It took awhile for me to see her as she really was, to recognize both ways in which she was victimized by a more powerful man and ways in which she colluded in that victimization because she also believed in patriarchy. Her continued acceptance of patriarchal thinking, even when there was a new way to see and do things, helped me to see she had agency and made choices. It helped me to see that at times she was coercive and cruel toward the children she had power over—that Dad could not be blamed for her actions. It was Mom, not Dad, who held all her girls in contempt if we did not embody her notions of the feminine ideal, her assumptions about beauty. She set the standards, she defined the parameters of how we would be punished if we did not measure up. Nancy Friday documents maternal sadism in her useful work *The Power of Beauty,* emphasizing our desperate denial and refusal to unmask idealized womanhood, especially when it comes to the mother-daughter relationship. Friday contends, "Until girls are raised from the beginning to feel there is great regard in becoming a unique individual, someone who is her mother's daughter but not her clone, we will go through life seeking other women's approval, fearing their disapproval." Maternal sadism and its impact on female self-esteem, the ways it inhibits female capacity to know love, remains a taboo subject. Patriarchy has blamed mothers for so much for so long that it is still difficult to critique mothers without reinforcing negative stereotypes.

Our cultural idealization of women as caregivers is so powerful. It's really one of the few positive traits assigned women by patriarchy. Therefore, it's not surprising that women are reluctant and at times downright unwilling to interrogate notions that we are inherently more loving. If this is the only positive characteristic females are allowed to claim, the one trait that lets us be seen as morally superior to men, most women will continue to be deeply invested in clinging to the perception that we are loving even when we know we are not. There is no doubt in my mind that it is easier for females of any age to learn the art of loving than it is for their male counterparts. It is easier because our interest in love is not questioned. To the extent that any woman takes the time and makes the choice to learn what love is, we are more supported in this endeavor than men are. More often than not the assumption that women naturally love more and better than men actually keeps us from facing our problems with love and intimacy. That's why so many of us only begin to learn what love really is in midlife.

It is awesome to consider how our culture and the meaning of love might have changed if instead of books like *Women Who Love Too Much* and *Men Are from Mars, Women Are from Venus* we were reading about women loving well and why. Rather than reading more woman-blaming literature in the guise of self-help, we would be focusing our hearts and minds on what really matters. It matters that women face our reality head-on, without lies and pretense. What woman does not hear the truth in Lerner's reminding us that as females (straight or gay) searching for love "few of us evaluate a prospective partner with the same objectivity and clarity that we might use to select a household appliance or a car." If women were well schooled in the art of loving, this would not be the case.

Concurrently, since women do more parenting than men and despite feminist change remain the primary caregivers, we need to investigate what the correlation is between this role and what we actually teach children about love. Do female parents teach children values or is that work done by school, television, and the like? Surely, if women value love so much, children, boys as well as girls, would be taught to value loving. In general, women do not see themselves as the guardians of ethics and values. While many women passionately desire to love and be loved, most of us, like the rest of the culture, see that desire as not worthy of serious attention and study.

Women, more so than men, spend an astounding amount of money to learn more about the nature of intimacy, to learn ways to make relationships work. Yet we have erected no schools of love, no think tanks that help us understand love better, nor have we created a diverse, large body of insightful writing on the subject. The time has come for women who are genuinely and passionately concerned with love to insist that love be valued in our culture. That insistence must stem concretely from the willingness to acknowledge our historical role in the devaluation of love. It must be grounded in an absolute refusal of sexist stereotypes that falsely tell us that females are inherently more loving than males, and in an absolute willingness to do the work of love, no matter how difficult, no matter the sacrifice.

When Jane Jervis entered consciousness-raising groups, she began "to realize that I was entitled to know how I liked my tuna fish and even to have it that way, and that if I wanted to have tuna fish the way I liked it, I was probably going to have to fix it myself." She entered graduate school at age thirty-four, a divorced mother (as she put it, "he wasn't thrilled by my new enthusiasms"), and got her Ph.D. at age forty. And guess what? She found herself, and because she was emotionally ready, she found mutual love.

Let's not kid ourselves, we find mutual love only when we know how to love. And the best place to start practicing the art of loving is with the self—that body, mind, heart, and soul that we can most know and change.

The one person who will never leave us, whom we will never lose, is ourself. Learning to love our female selves is where our search for love must begin. We begin this journey to love by examining the ideas and beliefs we have held about the nature of intimacy and true love. Rather than embracing faulty thinking that encourages us to believe that females are inherently loving, we make the choice to become loving. Choosing love, we affirm our agency, our commitment to personal growth, our emotional openness.

Eight

grow into a woman's body
and love it

ANY woman eager to learn the art of loving can start, as the Buddhist teachers say, "right where you are" by being self-loving. Nothing belies the assumption that women are more loving than men as much as the negative feelings most females hold about our bodies. One might easily argue that when it comes to learning self-love, men are moving in the right direction faster than women, because so many males unconditionally accept and like the bodies they inhabit. Let's face it, as a culture we are much more willing either to affirm male physicality or to relegate it to its proper place when determining overall value and worth.

Females easily endorse a mind-body split that lets us cultivate the false assumption that we can hate our bodies and still be loving. And not only do we embrace this faulty logic, but also the culture lets us get away with thinking that we can hate our bodies and still be seen as the group most capable of teaching others about love. Or, better yet, that we can hate our bodies and manifest positive self-esteem. From time to time a mother will approach me about her young daughter's self-hatred, wanting to know what she should do. I sense agitation and the desire to flee when I begin to ask the mother questions about how she feels about *her* self, *her* body, *her* being. Many mothers want to believe that if they just put the right images on the wall, buy the right books and wardrobe, and say affirming things, then their girl children will feel good about themselves.

We do not learn merely by what parents say; we learn by what they do. A parent who reassures a girl child that she is fine "just as she is" and who then repeatedly downgrades herself and other female peers is not laying the groundwork for healthy body self-esteem. Fathers who fret over young daughters who are overly obsessed with staying or becoming thin, telling them all that matters is being healthy even as they continually badger their female partners to lose weight and evaluate other women based on weight are actually promoting female self-hatred. Their daughters are not fooled. They get the message that being thin will determine their value, that it will be a crucial determinant of whether they will be loved.

In her amazing memoir, *Appetites,* Geneen Roth confesses, "Being thin was the magic that was supposed to
heal the damage at the core of me, the damage symbolized
by fat. If I lost the weight, I'd lose the damaged core."
Roth understands intimately the connection between the
female search for love and our obsession with being thin.
She writes that "our fantasy of what will happen when we
turn a final corner and find the love, respect, visibility, and
abundance that's eluded us for a lifetime . . . is the adult
version of the childhood longing to be seen and loved.
When as children we understand that we are going to get
that love, we make up stories, create a fantasy life, try to
be someone else. And when we believe that love will be
waiting around the corner if only we could transform ourselves into different people, we spend our lives trying to
turn that corner." This is self-hatred in action. Female self-
love begins with self-acceptance.

Women striving to raise daughters in families where
female bodies are unconditionally accepted, affirmed, and
admired can offer the best testimony about the ways constant bombardment of mass-media messages aimed at
teaching girls to dislike their physical beings abound.
Overall cultural devaluation of the female body affects the
self-esteem of all girls, even those who are raised in loving
homes. Constant vigilance is required to protect female
body self-esteem.

Grown women raised to hate their bodies can change

their minds. And they can change their minds at any age. They can begin to do the work of becoming self-loving by first reclaiming the right to inhabit a healthy body and to identify that as the foundation of beauty and attractiveness. This is one of those cultural revolutions that can take place just by our saying no. What we must say no to is a world that tells us we are solely defined by our physical bodies, that these female bodies are inadequate, lacking, and not good enough. Saying no to any devaluation and debasement of the female body is a loving practice.

The truth is not that it is hard or impossible to say no to our cultural obsession with female beauty as artifice, as something a female acquires by buying the right outfit or the latest product, but that most women have no desire to say no to artifice. Since we are endlessly told by mass media that our body self-hatred in no way makes us less desirable, more prone to depression and other life-threatening illnesses, or less likely to find love, there is no ongoing collective rebellion. One of the most vital aspects of contemporary feminism was its demand that women revolt against standards of beauty that require females to embrace life-threatening habits of being. Sadly, even though this focus on female body self-hatred brought eating disorders into the limelight, its impact was diminished as more and more powerful women, especially those who had been advocates of feminist politics, continued to embrace conventional woman-hating standards of beauty—

the primary one being unhealthy weight loss and the emphasis on being thin. Many women, whose only knowledge of feminist theory and practice came from mass media, naively assumed that feminists were vehemently opposed to the notion that women should look good and enjoy adornment. In reality, the feminist call was for women to embrace ways of seeing beauty and adorning ourselves that are healthy, life-affirming, and not overly time-consuming.

This revolt failed to change the attitudes and habits of masses of women. Its most positive impact on the fashion industry was felt in the demand that designers create beautiful, comfortable shoes that did not hurt or deform the feet for women to wear on all occasions. That fashion revolution worked. High-heeled shoes, the quintessential stiletto, are most assuredly making a comeback, but women in general exercise their right to buy shoes that are both comfortable and glamorous. Despite the feminist movement, many women continue to feel that it is unfeminine to have large feet. Most women buy shoes several sizes too small. They walk around in pain. Or they do not walk. They cannot love their feet. And yet our feet plant us on Earth, and the well-being of our feet is the ground we must stand on if we would be self-loving. Early on in the feminist movement we called attention to the female foot and the shoes offered us by designers who for the most part would never walk an inch, let alone a mile, in female shoes. Women need to remember the importance of caring for the well-being of our feet.

We know less about the folks that design shoes than we do about the folks that design clothes. Most clothing for women is still designed by men who are more enchanted by outfits that in no way meet the needs of real women or express our fantasies. Sexist women are still willing to let even more sexist men shape their fantasies and adorn them in ridiculous-looking outfits. Television shows like *Sex and the City* depict young professional women wearing clothing to work that is hyperfeminized and revealing. These young, supposedly powerful females are decked out in stiletto heels, plunging necklines, and tight clothes. Unfortunately, these images are trendsetting. On the positive side, some fashion magazines now display a mix of clothing. Clothes that are useful yet elegant and beautiful are shown with clothes that are utterly impractical, hysterically glamorous, and that sometimes border on the just plain ridiculous. Importantly, women now have a choice. The more self-loving we are, the more we can make choices that will enhance our unique, individual bodies and beings.

Since the feminist revolution to give us all the right to unconditionally affirm, accept, and admire the female body was not sustained, returning to this project is crucial if we are to create a meaningful cultural foundation in which females can learn to love our bodies. We need a feminist revolution wherein there would be exciting new fashion magazines offering glamorous images of women with great style, taste, and healthy bodies. One such magazine that already exists is *Mode,* which affirms the gorgeous, sensual beauty of big, attractive, healthy female bodies. Lamenting the prevalence of eating disorders, constantly exposing the horror, does little to change the way the vast majority of females think about beauty. Women who are daily dieting, starving themselves, or spending half their lives in gyms to keep their bodies thin, speak out against eating disorders. The contradictions are blatant and disgusting. When leading feminist thinkers tell girls and women to see our bodies as ourselves and love them but show that they themselves worship at the throne of thinness by refusing to eat, by endlessly dieting, their actions speak louder than their words.

Female obsession with thinness, female body hatred, is not something we can blame on men. More often than not, females are the body fascists who police themselves and other females with a brutal harshness that knows no bounds. Before many of us had ever looked at a fashion magazine or even cared how men saw us, hard and brutal body shaming began in our families. These crimes against our female body image were most often perpetrated by mothers, grandmothers, sisters, and other female relatives.

Despite his patriarchal power, in my home my father rarely commented on the appearance of any of his six daughters. It was our mom who told us how we should look, who berated us if we looked bad by whatever standards she chose to invoke at the moment. She felt that our appearance was a reflection of her worth and value. If we did not look good, she did not look good.

Not enough work has been done on females' parenting of females. If women are socialized within patriarchy to view all other females as potential threats, as competitors, then we have to consider again and again the ways such thinking shapes and informs mother-daughter bonds. Research indicates that young girls experience themselves as powerful and enjoy their bodies until the onset of puberty. At that time an indoctrination process begins to take place in which they learn to fear their flesh, to think it must be altered in some way in order to be acceptable or desirable. Mass-media and peer-group pressure are not the sole agents of this indoctrination; parents play a role. Given the homophobic, gay-hating thrust of our culture, many parents, male and female, feel it is their responsibility to urge the physically energetic, unashamed young female body to conform to sexist stereotypes of femininity. Colluding with the larger patriarchal culture, parents, especially mothers who fear being blamed, may deem it important to encourage girl children to become interested in conventional ways of producing beauty.

To some extent this focus on outer beauty is meant to cover up the inner changes occurring in the adolescent female body. In patriarchal culture these changes are often the breeding ground for self-hatred. Girls who may have liked themselves in their younger days enter adolescence with profound self-loathing. Again, despite the positive changes created by the feminist movement, most girls still experience feelings of shame, revulsion, disgust, and/or embarrassment when menstruation begins. Studies of pubescent girls show that they hate the idea of bleeding. They feel it makes them outcasts or potential objects of teasing and scorn. Advertisements associated with menstruation reinforce the notion that a female is in danger during this time of seriously damaging her self-image. Only rigorous protection can save her. Many young girls have already learned to hate their genitals even before the onset of menstruation, but, as Nancy Friday writes in *The Power of Beauty*, this is where "the self-loathing begins in earnest, genital abhorrence inherited from her mother who learned it from her mother." Progressive feminist women who have been determined to raise their daughters without body shame often find themselves in conflict with other parents and school officials who promote sex-negative thinking about the female body.

One of my friends tells her five-year-old daughter that her genitals are full of wonder and power. She found herself in the midst of controversy when her daughter shared this information with other girl children. Most parents still think it's taboo to speak openly about female genitalia, despite graphic depictions of naked bodies and sexual acts on prime-time television. Boys may fare better than girls because their potty-training years have usually included positive affirmation of their genitals. An episode of *Sex and the City* dramatized female fear and embarrassment about female genitals. In this episode, sexually adventurous and promiscuous Samantha, and the lead character, Carrie, encourage their friend, prim, conservative Charlotte, to look at her vagina in a mirror. Charlotte's perception of her vagina as ugly is transformed. She looks at her private parts with wide-eyed wonder and awe-inspiring reverence. In another episode, Charlotte celebrates her body by posing for a painting of her vagina. If these positive representations were tied to an overall celebration of the female body in all its forms, this show would be incredibly radical. Like our culture as a whole, it sends women a contradictory message: Love your body but make sure you starve it so that you can be thin and beautiful.

More than ever before, we recognize that there is a link between female hatred of the vagina, of menstrual bleeding, and female obsession with thinness. Anorexic girls and women often stop bleeding altogether. Testimony from young adult females who were raised to think of their genitals as a positive site of health, pleasure, and female beauty is the best documentation there is that women have the power to change negative attitudes about our bodies. Nancy Friday urges women to forge an all-out campaign to change attitudes toward menstrual cycles, writing, "We raise our daughters to believe that they can accomplish anything but saddle them with our miseries regarding menstruation. . . . I believe that no physical handicap inhibits women more than the mindset regarding the bleeding female body." Changing attitudes toward the female body, toward female genitalia, was a much-discussed aspect of the feminist movement early on. It may have ceased because the women who were putting these issues forward found both that it was quite easy to change their attitudes and create a positive perspective, as many of them were moving toward the stage of their lives when menstruation would cease.

At times it is both frightening and tragically ironic that we have more awareness of these issues as a nation than ever before and yet so little has changed. That awareness is a direct result of positive, life-affirming aspects of the feminist movement, yet it is not linked with either a sustained profeminist agenda or overall efforts in the culture as a whole to teach greater appreciation of female bodies. In fact, many people, especially women, act as though the feminist movement was only a negative rebellion, that it had no positive impact. Yet it was the feminist movement that increased cultural awareness of female body self-hatred, of life-threatening eating disorders, of dangerous cosmetic surgeries that damage the health of our bodies. Since all these concerns, first raised by feminist thinkers, were appropriated by mainstream focus on gender, it is much too easy for everyone to forget that awareness of problems alone is not a solution. To solve the problem of female body self-hatred, we have to critique sexist thinking, militantly oppose it, and simultaneously create new images, new ways of seeing ourselves.

Heightened awareness often gives the illusion that a problem is lessening. This is most often not the case. It may mean simply that a problem has become so widespread it can no longer remain hidden or be ignored. Despite all our public knowledge and awareness of eating disorders, young girls are increasingly likely to become addicted to controlling their weight in order to remain thin. That addiction sets the stage for eating disorders. More often than not, females who offer public testimony about the pain and horror they underwent as they share recovery stories are shown to be thin as the wind. We are supposed to assume that the glamorous thinness presented is no longer problematic. The contradictions here are obvious. If one were naturally thin, then the desire to starve oneself to become thin or to maintain thinness would be unnecessary. Obsessive control of weight is usually a response to the fear of gaining weight.

As we approach midlife, many women do gain weight. It is no accident that a large majority of women begin to rethink and let go of our obsession with thinness as we age. This is often the time in a woman's life when she begins to seriously evaluate and critique the values that have shaped her life. Successful aging women are much more acutely aware of sexism, of what must be done to challenge it at home and in the workplace in midlife. I hear myself and other women talk about the need to lose weight to appear more attractive to men at one moment, and then later in the same conversation critique that assumption. When I was thin anorexically and had difficulty eating, I had far fewer partners than during the years when I began to see health as seductive and attractive, when I chose to be healthy and to affirm and admire that as the most vital sign of beauty. Geneen Roth shares the insight that "weight has made no difference in the quality of love in my life—ever." And yet it was still difficult for her to let go of the assumption that thinness would make her more desirable, more worthy of love.

The mass media are much more interested in sharing stories of female body self-hatred than in depicting women who love their bodies just the way they are. We are much more likely to open a magazine and see an image of an aging woman looking way younger than her years, her body most closely resembling that of an adolescent girl, the article maybe even telling us the dietary and exercise regime that keeps her in shape, than to see gorgeous aging women with flesh on their bones. The vast majority of us have flesh on our bones. I wish I could report that we all love that flesh. Some of us do. Most of us do not. A great many of us simply give up, engaging in a process of negative acceptance. By that I mean that an individual woman may not like her looks, her weight, but ceases trying to change herself so that she no longer conforms to conventional sexist aesthetic standards, because to do so lessens her anxiety and stress. But she is still not self-loving. We cannot negate our bodies and love them.

The absence of a love-based value system leads women to continually make perceptions about appearance the major factor in self-esteem. Learning how to love ourselves includes rethinking negative attitudes toward the female body. With love we are able to celebrate healthy bodies, placing beauty and adornment in their proper perspective. When females turn our search for love in the direction of our own bodies, we can collectively create a cultural revolution wherein the fundamental connection between loving one's body and being self-loving will be obvious.

Until women break through denial and recognize that we have the power to positively change our perceptions of the female body, we will always be missing out on love. If someone loves us but we are trapped by self-hatred, their love will never reach us. We will question it, devalue it, be like the heroine of Nikki Giovanni's "Woman Poem," who declares, "i ain't shit you must be lower / than that to care." Affirming our natural beauty before we adorn it in other ways keeps us from developing a dependency on artifice. It safeguards our body self-esteem. Think of all the women you know who will not allow themselves to be seen without makeup. I often wonder how they feel about themselves at night when they are climbing into bed with intimate partners. Are they overwhelmed with secret shame that someone sees them as they really are? Or do they sleep with rage that who they really are can be celebrated or cared for only in secret? For years I never wore makeup. Then, in my forties, I began to wear lipstick, which I continue to enjoy with a child's delight. But for a time that enjoyment ceased when I began to feel as though I was not bright enough, not visible enough without this color on my lips. I wanted to feel as good about my looks without lipstick as I felt with it. And I was the one in control of my perceptions. I was the one who could affirm both gestures.

All women dream of meeting a partner who will like our bodies as they are. We long for partners who will offer affirmation and unconditional acceptance, particularly if we have never been affirmed or were affirmed only as children in our families of origin. We long for acceptance of our physical beings, to be admired as we are, even as we withhold affirmation from ourselves. This is the worst form of self-sabotage. We can "start where we are" by offering ourselves that gaze of approval we long to see in the eyes of someone else. The more we love our flesh, the more others will delight in its bounty. As we love the female body, we are able to let it be the ground on which we build a deeper relationship to ourselves—a loving relationship uniting mind, body, and spirit.

sisterhood: love and solidarity

M OST women search for love hoping to find recognition of our value. It may not be that we do not see ourselves as valuable; we simply do not trust our perceptions. When I was a girl, I thought I had marvelous traits. I was perpetually surprised that so much that I believed was grand and delightful in myself was hateful and suspect in the eyes of my parents, especially my mother. Still, she was full of contradictions. One day my mother might mock my love of reading and threaten to take all the books away, and another day she might speak with pride about the same passions that had been previously mocked, used to shame and humiliate me.

In her book *Life and Death: Unapologetic Writings on the Continuing War Against Women,* Andrea Dworkin describes her mother's telling her often "that she loved me but did not like me." Women of all races and classes offer testimony of being told this by their mothers. Its impact was to make them feel as though something was deeply wrong about them. Describing her relationship with her mother, Dworkin recalls, "She experienced my inner life as a reproach. She thought I was arrogant and especially hated that I valued my own thoughts. When I kept what I was thinking to myself, she thought I was plotting against her. When I told her what I thought, she said I was defiant and some species of bad: evil, nasty, rotten. She often accused me of thinking I was smarter than she." Again and again I hear testimony from gifted women about their mothers' accusations of arrogance. My mother continually berated me for what she perceived to be my thinking that I was smarter and better than she.

Feminist scholarship has helped us to understand that women who suppress their own unique gifts in the interest of being dutiful daughters, wives, and mothers are often filled with rage. Whereas it would seem logical that a woman who feels thwarted in her own development might be thrilled to see her daughter become actualized, all too often her eroded self-esteem leads to mixed feelings or full-on expressions of competition and rage. At its worst this mother-daughter warfare may actually lead parents to commit acts of soul murder, wherein they systematically try to destroy a daughter's self-esteem so that her gifts will never be realized.

Patriarchal thinking normalizes competition between mothers and daughters, as well as the girl child's rebellion. Luckily, progressive feminist mothers who have either unlearned cripplingly low self-esteem or who were provident enough to be raised in families where their growth was nurtured are daily raising wonderful daughters without competing with or devaluing them. Their experience stands as direct challenge to any notion that jealousy and competition are naturally present in mother-daughter bonds. In the presence of this group of self-loving girls, our woman spirit is uplifted. Their personal power is intoxicating and awesome. They exude it like a strong and heady perfume. And it is easy to see how such girlhood power, were it widespread, could easily undermine the conventional sexist social order. One day these girls will become women who will publicly tell their stories. Their memories of supporting, affirming, consistently caring mothers will stand as a counternarrative challenging and changing the old images of mother-daughter hatred and conflict.

Ugly competition and conflict between mothers and daughters is not simply the outcome of sexist suppression of adult women's growth and self-actualization. Plenty of talented, successful, powerful women compete in unkind and cruel ways with their daughters. Horror stories abound about the relationships between famous mothers and their daughters. While much attention was focused on the consensual sexual relationship between father and daughter in writer Kathyrn Harrison's memoir *The Kiss,* the really shocking story the book chronicles is the intense vicious rivalry between Harrison and her mother. In *Oranges Are Not the Only Fruit,* Jeanette Winterson's working-class mother punished her daughter for her passion for books. She worries that her mother will find the collection of books she has gathered, writing, "One day she did. She burned everything."

Some folks would argue that they parent as their mothers parented them; hence, sexist thinking continues to be a primary culprit. Importantly, this negative, competitive impulse, which seeks the psychic annihilation and destruction of the other, the female who possesses what one lacks, often characterizes mother-daughter bonds as well as general female interaction. Competition between successful women and their daughters is often rooted in the adult woman's fear of aging in a patriarchal culture. No matter how talented and powerful a woman is, the rules of sexism continue to render her valueless as she ages. Hence, a gifted, successful, attractive woman may feel threatened by the reality that sexism ensures that her daughter, who may be less gifted and not at all successful or attractive, will still "win" by being more valued by virtue of youth.

When I was an insecure young woman, I did not think

youthfulness was a resource. My shaky self-esteem made youth a burden. I wanted to grow older, for I was certain that with age would come clarity and confidence. Moving into midlife, I suddenly awakened one day to the reality of the power of a young woman's body in patriarchal culture. While I had known this intellectually, it was quite another matter to experience it deeply—viscerally. To be honest, it shocked me to realize I would never have access to this fresh, youthful energy again. I am convinced that older men desire younger women in part to siphon off this energy, not to have to deal with its permanent loss in their own lives. Clearly an aging woman with cripplingly low self-esteem easily feels such youthful energy to be an annihilating affront. And an insecure mother who has to witness the vibrancy of this emerging youthful womanness might see it solely as an attack on her identity and personhood.

Intense hatred and cruelty in mother-daughter bonds is described again and again in contemporary memoirs. While many readers were shocked by Kathryn Harrison's revelation of chosen father–adult daughter incest in her memoir *The Kiss,* I found her intense hatred of her mother to be shocking. Tragically, the hatred and competition between them seemed to motivate her acquiescence as a young adult to her father's inappropriate sexual overtures. Describing her childhood, growing up in the same house as both her mother and maternal grandmother, Harrison confesses she learned to repress her true feelings, "a lesson reinforced often during a childhood of female warfare and tricky, shifting alliances." Writing about her eating disorder, she further declares, "Anorexia may begin as an attempt to make myself fit my mother's ideal and then to erase myself, but its deeper, more insidious and lasting seduction is that of exiling her. Anorexia can be satisfied, my mother cannot; so I replace her with this disease, with a system of penances and renunciation that offers its own rewards. That makes mothers obsolete." While review after review of this book rhapsodized about the illicit "romance" between father and grown daughter, Harrison's monstrous hatred of her mother is perceived as "normal."

Writing retrospectively, Harrison suggests that her hatred of her mother is a justifiable response to maternal neglect and indifference. Yet her father had been absent, neglectful, and abusive, but he is never the object of her total rage, scorn, and contempt. Women find it easier to rage against one another. Anger directed at males feels more threatening, their power to retaliate more dangerous. Harrison's mother refuses to respond to her daughter's longing for consistent, caring recognition. Many of our mothers have behaved in this contradictory manner, but most of us do not retaliate against them with competitive rage and hatred. Feminist thinker Naomi Wolf, in her memoir *Promiscuities,* felt it was normal that she and her peers "nursed an emerging sexual competition with our mothers." In her recent memoir *Black, White, and Jewish,* Rebecca Walker chronicles her desperate longing to compete with the world of "fame" to capture the undivided attention of her writer mother.

I went through a phase in my young-adult life in which I longed to have a mother who was intellectually successful. My fantasy was that this mom could serve as a guide, showing me how to navigate my way through the turbulent waters of artistic development. If nothing else, I imagined we would talk together. This image of mother-daughter bonding was shattered for me as I began to meet the daughters of "famous" mothers. The grown daughter of a famous artist invited me to a showing of her new work and preceded to tell me that she had been sent makeup in the mail by her mother and told not to come "looking frumpy." She had also been told that she could bring a friend as long as we did not speak. A well-known thinker and writer, the daughter willingly acquiesced to her mother's demands, desiring both to please her and to avoid incurring her wrath.

Way too many of the mothers I met were either dangerously competitive or studiously indifferent. Hungry for their mothers' attention and approval, the daughters were often so emotionally fragile that they were incapable of making life-affirming decisions for themselves in either work or relationships. Most shocking to me was the reality that many of these successful moms were advocates of feminism. While they could brilliantly critique male sexism, they remained blind to how sexist notions of womanhood informed the way they related to their daughters, or, for that matter, to other women. Their brutal treatment of their daughters did not end in childhood but continued even as the girls became mature, wounded women. Writing about female response to her success when feminist movement was going strong, Erica Jong recalls, "I was shocked by the bitter criticism I received from some very smart women. . . . The number of feminists who attack other women is shocking! It seems to me that if women are going to change the world, they first have to change themselves and rise above that competitiveness, which we have been taught, and learn to be truly sisterly to each other."

Envy between females has always been brutally divisive. What woman among us does not remember the very first time she heard the story of Snow White or Hansel and Gretel? How many of us were puzzled by the hatred these older, more powerful women harbored toward innocent girls. I remember wondering why there had to be a constant contest to see who was "the fairest of them all." It was hard to comprehend that Hansel and Gretel were starved as their parents ate. And who could understand the father's allowing the mean wife/stepmother to cast them out? In a collection of essays written by women talking about the fairy tales that most affected us, Fern Kupfer emphasizes the impact that stories of competing, evil stepmothers had on her consciousness. Writing her memories in "Trust," she recalls, "It is the story of a child in the world without a mother, without resource or protection, that haunted me so in the fairy tales I read as a girl. Of abused Cinderella, isolated Rapunzel, of motherless Snow White . . ." These stories often serve as our girlhood indoctrination into the nature of relationships between women, between young girls and their female elders. Kupfer writes about rethinking the role of the stepmother when she became one. Whenever she was uncertain of how best to care for her stepdaughters, Kupfer would imagine how she would want a stepmother to treat her biological daughter if she were not in the picture. She let her answers to that question guide her.

The contemporary film version of *Snow White* was so troubling because the stepmother (magnificently portrayed by Sigourney Weaver) is very beautiful, yet her beauty is not enough. And in this film the stepdaughter has already decided not to give her new parent a chance. This movie made their female hatred of one another mutual. Their acts of brutality (attempting to burn each other or bury each other alive) were so bizarre as to be painful to watch. In many narratives of competition between females, especially where there is an age difference, youth wins out but affection between women is lost in the end. As everything goes up in flames, only the stench of envy remains.

Before it was cool simply to announce one's feminism,

women became feminists by undergoing a conversion process, usually through attending consciousness-raising groups. Contrary to popular myths that would have everyone believe that women in those groups did nothing but sit around bad-mouthing men, most of these groups began with women talking about how we saw ourselves and other women, how we acted. We openly confessed our fears and hatreds of other females. We talked about how to combat jealousy, the politics of envy, and so on. Part of the process of becoming a feminist was to critique and change our sexist ways of seeing one another. Sisterhood wasn't just about what we shared in common—things like periods, obsessive concern with our looks, or bitching about men—it was about women learning how to care for one another and be in solidarity, not just when we have complaints or when we feel victimized.

Lots of women can hang tight with one another and bond if one of them has a problem or if they share a problem. Affirming another woman's success is the difficult issue for many females, even those of us who claim to be feminists. From girlhood on, females learn how to use terroristic tactics of exclusion, ostracism, and shunning to police one another. Studies show that boys may fight with one another in competitive conflicts rooted in envy or jealousy but rarely employ long-range terroristic tactics to "ice" one another. Girls compete often to the death, and by that I mean to symbolic murder of one another. All this essentially woman-hating behavior continues into adulthood. It is woman-hating because it is rooted in the same fairy-tale logic that teaches us that only one female can win the day or be chosen. It is as though our knowledge that females lack value in the eyes of patriarchy means we can gain value only by competing with one another for recognition.

At one time it was believed that females did not know how to engage in healthy competition because we, unlike our male counterparts, did not learn this skill playing sports. Yet women who coach female competitive sports report that major difficulties arise when teammates disagree and that these interactions tend to be especially brutal. As a writer, I have found this to be equally the case, that when I am, or any woman is, perceived as getting more attention than her peers, she will be viciously attacked, not the media. And if she writes a lot, then women who write less will put her down or publicly say her work is repetitive. The list could go on. Particularly, women seem unable to acknowledge or value an individual woman who is perceived as being exceptional. Often other women will accuse her of being a fraud.

Apparently males are better socialized to accept that an individual man may have exceptional skills or talents. In the world of competitive sports, everyone will agree that Michael Jordan is an exceptional basketball player. Now, that does not mean that other gifted ballplayers will not strive to win against him, but when he scores more, they don't go around saying he is not really a good player, he is just lucky. The heart of female inability to affirm "exceptional" females is the threat of annihilation. On one hand, women in patriarchal culture confront what I euphemistically call "the Dixie cup mentality." This is that form of sexist thinking that says females are all alike, therefore, it does not matter which one you choose. Faced with this logic, some females feel that the way to compete is to identify flaws and lacks in other females. Since our unique, distinctive traits may not be acknowledged by patriarchy (and, most important, by the men in our lives—fathers, brothers, and, if we are heterosexual, lovers), then females may feel as though the only way to get special attention or to be chosen is by diminishing the value of female peers. It is a lot easier to cut down or trash someone else and harder to cultivate one's own special attributes.

When we, as females, cultivate our own attributes, we do the work of building the self-esteem that is the bedrock of self-love. While many books have been written on the subject I remain a great fan of Nathaniel Branden's *Six Pillars of Self-Esteem*. He defines these six pillars as the practice of living consciously, of self-acceptance, of self-responsibility, of self-assertiveness, of living purposefully, and of personal integrity. Of these, self-acceptance is particularly hard for females. Branden defines self-acceptance as the "refusal to be in an adversarial relationship to myself." Early on, in girlhood, most females learn to feel that we are flawed in some way that must be corrected. Whatever the ground of this notion, it is definitely, continually reinforced by sexism. This thinking automatically places us in an adversarial position with ourselves. Progressive therapy can help individuals move toward self-acceptance because it teaches us how to cease being our own worst enemy. Branden's use of the word "refusal" is crucial. Women need to claim our power to say no to all that negates our value.

Being affirming and self-accepting happens easily if we consciously practice refusing to embrace negative accounts of ourselves and our reality. One of the reasons many more women begin to be self-loving in midlife rather than at earlier stages of our growth is that it is a time when we feel free to please ourselves. The women interviewed in Beth Benatovich's collection *What We Know So Far* all testify that self-acceptance is easier. Billie Jean King enjoys the fact that in midlife "finally we can do anything we want . . . and that equates to freedom." Elizabeth Watson urges women in midlife to speak out: "Stand up for what you believe. Go back to that teenage person you were, who wanted something very badly, then go out and get it. This is a time in your life when there's nothing and no one standing in your way." After years of pleasing others or being self-effacing, women in midlife often begin to do the work of self-critique, an evaluation that might have been more difficult or threatening at a younger age.

We know in midlife that time is running out, that we will not have endless chances to start over. In Jane Jervis's story of how she set out on her path to becoming a college president in midlife, she acknowledged that choosing to value her needs led to the end of her first marriage. Women in longtime marriages whose husbands abandon them in midlife, often to choose a younger partner, frequently come face-to-face with the reality that they do not have an autonomous identity. Midlife marks the moment of their self-creation. My best friend, from my first year in college, divorced after more than twenty years of marriage, has raised four wonderful children, and is now doing the work of reclaiming the identity she established long ago but then surrendered in patriarchal marriage. Finding herself is a heady, thrilling experience. She has never been so free. And it's both exhilarating and frightening. Like many of us, she is coming to self-love late, but her journey has been full and rich.

Self-love is always risky for women within patriarchy. Females are rewarded more when we experience ourselves and act as though we are flawed, insecure, or especially dependent and needy. A woman who does not learn how first to fulfill her psychological needs for acceptance will always operate from a space of lack. This psychic state will make her vulnerable and will often lead her into unhealthy relationships. Although it is risky, when we are self-loving, our growing contentment and personal power sustains us when we are rejected or punished for refusing to follow conventional sexist rules. Usually, self-help books and therapies encourage us to believe that acts of self-love will make life better, happier. So it is especially confusing to women when we choose to be self-loving only to find ourselves resented.

In my sweetest period of self-recovery, when I felt I was finally embracing myself wholeheartedly, I was initially thrown off balance by the lack of positive response to these changes. It was as though people in my life liked me better when I was in crisis, not eating properly, or depressed. In graduate school I was always awed in the presence of successful, beautiful, older women who seemed to have everything; then I would later hear about their alcoholism or other self-destructive habits. Knowing that these women had serious problems mediated their power in the eyes of many of their peers. It made the hatred of their power less intense. Often they were the objects of pity. Had they been healthy, had they been perceived as really having it all, they would assuredly have been the objects of vicious envy and cruel attacks.

More men were attracted to me and to other women I knew when we were untogether. This is because it's easier to subordinate someone who does not feel good about herself or her life, or someone who may feel constantly insecure and afraid. Women readily testify that they stay in unhappy relationships because they fear no one else will want them. Instinctively, they know that the more able a woman is to assert agency on behalf of her well-being, the less desirable she may be in patriarchal culture. While fewer men may "want" women who are healthy and self-loving, bonds with these men who do are more affirming, constant, and fulfilling.

Concurrently, many women find themselves rejected by female pals when they make changes that differ from shared patterns of behavior that once bonded them together. Women often bond by sharing secrets and common experiences, lying about anything that would reveal differences in perspectives or desires. And it is often betrayal that breaks those bonds. Before women can create abiding love with one another, we must learn to be truth tellers, to break with the sexist notion that a good woman never tells what she really thinks. Many a friendship between women has ended because one person failed to speak her truths directly to her friend, choosing instead to inform her of her feelings through petty gossip and slander. In Harriet Lerner's useful work *The Dance of Deception*, she explains, "The struggle toward truth-telling is at the center of our deepest longing for intimacy with others. . . . Truth-telling cannot co-exist with inequality. . . . There is never a resting place in the struggle for personal and political integrity. . . . We can live today according to the values that we wish would govern the world in the hypothetical future we are working for. To honor diversity, complexity, inclusiveness, and connection in our lives now is to widen the path of truth-telling for everyone." Personal integrity is the foundation of self-love. Women who are honest with themselves and others do not fear being vulnerable. We do not fear that another woman can unmask or expose us. We need not fear annihilation, for we know no one can destroy our integrity as women who love.

No woman who chooses to be self-loving ever regrets her choice. Self-love brings her greater power and freedom. It improves her relationships with everyone. But most especially it allows her to live in community with other women, to stand in solidarity and sisterhood. Marilyn Frye shares this useful insight in her book of collected writings, *Willful Virgin*: "To make a difference . . . women have to do impossible things and think impossible thoughts, and that is only done in community. Without a community of sense, an individual cannot keep hold of her radical insights, she becomes confused, she forgets what she knew. . . . We call each other to creative acts of courage, imagination, and memory, but they are literally impossible without a community of women which recognizes and authorizes women's initiatives." While the self-loving woman may encounter more conflict, she has the skill to handle difficulties that come her way. That skill is grounded in self-acceptance, integrity, and a willingness always to do what is best for her well-being. Coupled with those skills, she has the strength to stand in community with women, to enter a circle of love.

Recently my best friend from undergraduate years visited me with her daughters. In their presence we celebrated more than thirty years of friendship, telling them all we did to nurture our bond. We shared our willingness to give each other the benefit of the doubt in difficult moments, like the time she wrongly imagined I was seducing her boyfriend or the time I was upset because she had not explained race and racism to her children, this oversight from a white woman whose best friend is black. We shared our ongoing commitment to being honest with each other, to forgiving, to nurturing our personal growth. We count ourselves lucky that our love abides, that it has stood the test of time and different choices.

April remembers my telling her when I was eighteen that I had no intentions of marrying, that I needed to be independent, a free woman. And she recalls feeling that same longing but somehow suppressing it and letting the culture pull her into marriage when she had not yet fully claimed herself. We can speak our differences, sharing the little envy we may feel about each other's lives (yes, I envy her having such wonderful daughters), and yet that envy need not turn into negative jealousy, for she lets me share in her bounty. At this moment of union we toasted female friendship, love, and solidarity, and hope for her girls that they, too, will find a circle of love in which to dance, a body of women whose arms will always hold and embrace them. We wanted to share our wisdom so that they will come to self-love sooner than we did, so that they will love other women rightly.

In the church I attended while growing up, one of my favorite songs posed the question "Is it well with your soul, are you free and made whole?" When we are self-loving, we attend to the deeper needs of our soul, we no longer fear abandonment or loss of recognition. We see ourselves clearly as we really are. And that clarity is the source of our strength and peace of mind. It is the space of mindful awareness where we can search for love together, communing and celebrating, cherishing the sweetness of sustained female solidarity.

Ten

our right to love

WOMEN cannot live by self-love alone. I dare to make that proclamation in response to the barrage of advice-giving material in self-help books that pits self-love against our needs to love and be loved by others. Truly no woman can fully receive love without first being self-loving. Undoubtedly, in a male-centered, woman-hating culture, there is such ongoing demand that females be self-negating, placing pleasing others above self-development, that advocates for women's well-being are often driven to the other extreme. Insisting on both the need and the right of women to be self-loving, they make it seem as though once this happens we will all "live happily ever after" and therefore should not waste our precious time longing for the love of our dreams, for partnerships.

In reality, females of all ages who either learn how to love as children (and consequently are self-loving) or learn how to be self-loving later in life often confront major difficulties, because our culture has not yet been transformed in ways to support and sustain female well-being. If that were the case, our collective lack of self-love and self-esteem would not be a problem. Often, especially for adult women, the choice to be self-loving requires tremendous sacrifice. This is especially true if prior to doing the work of self-love everyone in their lives were accustomed to devaluing and/or subordinating them. Acknowledging this helps us understand why masses of women who may intuitively know that they need to do the work of self-love are trapped by fear.

Significant changes mean we have to confront loss. Whenever we give up something, there is a gap—even if what we are giving up needs to go. Usually we will go through a period of depression. The women interviewed in Beth Benatovich's collection *What We Know So Far: Wisdom Among Women* all talk about struggling to move through fear to embrace change. Japanese-American writer Janice Mirikitani comments, "Change is not easy for most people. Often a bad reality is preferable to the idea of change; we prefer to embrace the demons we know than the positive force we don't know." The fact that so many women choose to stay stuck is one explanation for why they, along with the larger society, may be especially distrustful, suspicious of, or attacking toward women who are fully self-actualized and loving of themselves and others.

Being successful is not synonymous with being self-loving. Gloria Steinem's bestselling book *Revolution from Within* exposed the extent to which many women achieved success who continued to lack fulfillment because of persistent low self-esteem. The more women strive to achieve, the more we confront the need to create positive self-esteem and self-love. Steinem reminds us, "Indeed, when core self-esteem remains low even into adulthood, no amount of external task-oriented achievement or approval seems able to compensate." Without this positive foundation, at some point (and this was a major thesis of Steinem's book) low self-esteem will undermine us. A dimension of the low self-esteem some successful women cannot shake is the fear that choosing to achieve means that they are automatically not "feminine" or less desirable. These feelings may persist even when these women have meaningful, committed relationships and/or marriages. In my role as a professor I continue to be disturbed by the presence of brilliant female students in the classrooms who do not wish to soar for fear that they will place themselves out of love's reach.

I was so happy when I entered a committed relationship at nineteen, because I felt that once I had proven I could get a man, I could turn my attention to developing my intellectual and artistic abilities. The relief I felt was enormous. It was as though I had removed a heavy weight off me. Throughout my growing-up years I had been repeatedly told by parents and teachers alike that men did not really like smart women, that by choosing to strive for higher education I was making myself even less desirable. As soon as I found a male peer who validated my intellect, I bonded with him. The issue of desire and partnership out of the way (for once I had a male companion, I had proven myself worthy of love—that I was not a failure), I could concentrate on other aspirations. Yet I still felt terribly insecure inside. That insecurity did not leave me until I did the work of learning how to be self-loving. The work of self-love began with self-acceptance. To accept myself fully I needed to heal from childhood wounds caused by traumatic abuse. Progressive therapy and feminist consciousness-raising groups were the setting wherein I learned to break with the past and create more positive futures.

My longtime relationship ended just when I had finished my doctorate and was taking a teaching job at a prestigious Ivy League institution. Even though I chose to end the relationship, my choice was motivated by my partner's refusal to wholeheartedly support and affirm my achievements. All during graduate school one of my student friends had teased me that the moment I was offered a job, my relationship would end. She felt that my partner's willingness to affirm my intellect did not mean anything as long as my intellectual aspirations were just that, aspirations. Graduate school had been difficult for me. I found it to be similar to the dysfunctional patriarchal family wherein I had been the object of repeated, abusive shaming and rites of humiliation. It took me a long while to finish my degree. Through all this time my male partner offered more support and encouragement than anyone had given me before. When he withdrew that support at the moment of my success, I was shocked and disappointed. I felt as though all the patriarchal prophecies handed down by parents and teachers had been revealed, that in the end men really did not like smart women. These sentiments are echoed in many autobiographical narratives by women striving to succeed. And indeed, women had warned me repeatedly that my male partner was not bothered by my intelligence as long as he could be the superior mentor figure and I his sexy, rebellious protégée, but that my excelling, moving beyond him, would lead to rejection. And when he took away his support at critical moments, I irrationally felt that I must have done something wrong.

Many women have had this experience, especially women who move from sexist sex roles to liberatory habits of being. Born in China, Korean acupuncturist and herbologist Ai Ja Lee married a pharmacy-school classmate who, though initially supportive, felt undermined by her success when she began to be recognized as having exceptional skill as a healer. He responded with violence and betrayal. When they took the pharmacy exams after immigrating to New York and she passed on the first try and he did not, he wanted a divorce. Lee recalls, "I never thought he was a bad man—just frightened and feeling inferior to his wife, which hurt his pride. . . . So he left, taking the car and the furniture with him. I had three dollars left, and three babies to support. I was so ashamed to be left this way . . . that I thought seriously about committing suicide." Most women striving to achieve who are emotionally abandoned by their partners hear some familiar tape playing in their head blaming them for the end of the relationship, as though their desire for success created the problem, rather than the sexism of their partners. Blaming themselves for the failure of relationships takes away from the joy and confidence they should be feeling about career advancement.

Once women proved ourselves to be the equals of men in the workplace, strategies to undermine this success were intensified. Not only did sexist thinkers, male and female, continue to promote the idea that these women were man-hating and unfeminine because they desired achievement, they were then portrayed as utterly monstrous and demonic. Represented as more ruthless and predatory than their male counterparts, they were "bitch goddesses." In keeping with the spirit of being woman-loving, feminist thinkers denounced this stereotypical construction of powerful women, calling attention to the ways this form of backlash was directed at discouraging women from striving to be high achievers. Feminist thinkers pointed out the ways a woman in charge will often be perceived as "difficult" even though she may be doing her job using the same skills and strategies her male peers use. While a man who is blunt, rigorous, and to the point is likely to be perceived as decisive and capable, a woman with those same skills will be described as bitchy and aggressive. Likewise, a powerful, charismatic woman who attracts attention will often be described as exhibitionist, as "sucking the air out of any room she enters." I had never heard this expression before until a colleague and peer used it to describe another woman who she felt was getting too much attention. Having heard it once, I began to hear it used often as a way of describing powerful, talkative women.

The image of a powerful woman as suffocating others, by taking away the very air they breathe, is a monstrously violent representation. Playing upon the image of women as the givers of life, this image evokes the notion of perverted womanhood. Not only, then, is the powerful woman not a nurturer, she is confined always to the role of predator, one who gets pleasure in taking life. I find it disturbing that in every case where I have heard this phrase used, it has been evoked by a woman to put down and trash another woman. Like so many negative representations of powerful women, the underlying implication of this image is the notion that women who seek power and success cannot be loving or life-affirming. By choosing to be powerful, they are automatically positioning themselves outside a matrix wherein they will be perceived as women who can give and receive love.

Despite rigorous and ongoing feminist challenges to negative, stereotypical, sexist images of powerful women, particularly high achievers, these images prevail. The intensity of their hold on mass culture's imagination is so strong that many young women seeking to be independent, powerful, and successful have simply embraced the idea that they are "bitches." Their uncritical acceptance of this image is problematic. It helps perpetuate sexist stereotypes about powerful women. Young women want to embrace the "hard bitch" image because it keeps them from having to confront the pain that comes when females are punished for choosing to be self-actualized and successful. Even though it may require daring for a female to transgress boundaries and disrupt the image of femininity that would have us all be "good girls," this transgression does not place her outside the traditional sexist norms. It is those traditional sexist norms that divide women into Madonna or whore, saintly nurturer or bitch goddess. A female who chooses to be a bitch is actually choosing to stay within the boundaries sexism has prescribed for us;

she is neither a genuine rebel nor a revolutionary. She is merely capitulating to the sexist notion that to be powerful she must be a bitch.

Elizabeth Wurtzel's book *Bitch: In Praise of Difficult Women* is the most glaring example of a successful young woman's public embrace of the bitch persona. In her introduction, titled "manufacturing fascination," she declares, "Obviously, in the pagentry of public life, in the places where women invent personae, the one statement a girl can make to declare her strength, her surefootedness, her autonomy—her self as a *self*—is to somehow be bad, somehow do something that is surely going to make her parents weep." Contrary to Wurtzel's pronouncement, it is obvious to most girls and women that to act on the behalf of our deepest longing for self-expression usually places us at odds with the culture, and that includes parents, whether we want to be bad or not.

When I rebelled against my parents, who did not want me to attend Stanford University because it was so far away from home, I did not do so happily, to declare defiance. I wanted and needed their support. Going against their wishes was frightening and psychologically upsetting. Then and now I want to live in a world where every female can make choices to grow spiritually and intellectually without having to resist in ways that increase our isolation and insecurity. I resented having to mature in a world that was eager to make every act of female self-love appear to be a gesture of selfishness, every act of assertiveness a mark of the bitch. Wurtzel may feel that "the bitch as role model, as icon and idea, has moments of style and occasions of substance," but the truth remains that few women benefit from bitchiness. While performing in the bitch persona may be fun for a while, in time it merely ensures that a woman will suffer old patterns of punishment designed to make certain that the bitch will not only know her place but also stay in her place. And the bitchiness of a youthful, sexy woman who has not come into her full power is much more tolerated than is a fully grown, mature bitch, who is usually scorned, punished, hated. No self-loving woman wants to be a bitch. And seeing other women as bitches just keeps alive the sexist notion that pathology is the order of the day whenever a woman transgresses the status quo.

Embracing the bitch persona is by definition a repudiation of the idea that powerful women need to receive love. Young women who think it's cool to be dubbed a bitch see dissing love as a badge of honor. Aping patriarchal men who deny the importance of emotional growth and care, they sport a "hard" persona. Whether young or older, women who are content with claiming the bitch category are still living in the woman hating domain of sexism. Rather than helping to clear the path for all females to claim our selfhood with courage and grace, they aid the patriarchy by supporting the sexist assumption that the choice to be fully self-actualized makes one a bitch.

Being self-loving utterly eliminates the possibility that a woman will choose to embrace negative categories as a sign of power. Even though there may be occasions when assertive behavior is seen by others as "bitchy," liberated women know the difference between constructive response and rude actions. No one expects the bitch-goddess women who are high achievers or hard-core, stay-at-home manipulators to be loving. Indeed, the assumption is that women who are striving for self-expression, power, and success are lacking in both knowledge of love and desire to love.

Popular culture consistently sends the message to females, and everyone else, that successful career women are failures when it comes to love. One of the most powerful forces undermining working women has been mass media's representation of the working "feminist" career woman as narcissistically self-centered and evil. From the construction of the career woman as evil and murderous in *Fatal Attraction* to the seemingly more benign image of the divorced working mom in a family movie like *One Fine Day* or the ad executive in the more recent *What Women Want*, the message continues to be that women who are high achievers are psychologically messed up. And whether or not we love or are loved is the arena in which we must once again prove that we are worthy, that we are still desirable and therefore feminine.

Not only did the movie *Fatal Attraction* perpetuate the

notion that the powerful, single, professional woman is trying to be a man (she is called Alex), but it also depicted this woman as unable to understand how to love in a healthy manner because she has been given "feminine qualities." Viciously murdered by the feminine good wife and mother who embodies sexist notions of perfect womanhood, Alex is punished because she has chosen to repudiate sexist norms. Her search for love is portrayed as a mad and maddening quest. Since the patriarchal message of the movie is that Alex could have found love if she had just stayed in the place of the sexist-defined feminine ideal, audiences are encouraged to see her as inviting punishment. In *The Seven Stories of Love,* author Marcia Millman remembers that audiences were happy to witness the murder of Alex, played by actress Glenn Close: "When I first saw *Fatal Attraction,* many people in the move theater cheered when [Michael] Douglas's wife kills Glenn Close before she can stab her husband. Few people expressed any sympathy for Close's character—she had turned into a monster, and we don't like to see how capable we are of monstrous behavior." Alex will go down in our nation's film history as one of the most hated female cinematic figures. No wonder, then, that in the twenty-first century the female advertising executive in *What Women Want* does not protest or resist her fate but waits until she is given permission by the macho corporate male predator–turned–feminist to meekly state the profound truth that what she

wants is to be liked for who she is, to be accepted as someone who is both smart and lovable. She does not want to
be seen as a bitch.

When the notion that all powerful women can do is
embrace the identity of bad-girl bitch converges with
unenlightened feminist assumptions that it undermines our
power for successful women to express emotional needs,
the female search for love is deemed pathological. It is seen
as a sign of failure or weakness. In actuality, powerful
women reveal psychological wholeness when we refuse to
embrace any type of thinking that suggests we should or
must choose success over love. Powerful, self-loving women
know that our ability to take care of our emotional needs
is essential, but this does not take the place of loving fel-
lowship and partnership. Many single successful women in
midlife feel there are few places where we can talk openly
about our desire to have loving partnerships without being
seen as desperate or, worse, as needing pity. I found again
and again that if I talked openly about the importance of
giving and receiving love in my life, especially about my
desire to have a partner, these feelings were ridiculed or
mocked. Surprisingly, colleagues and friends would often
suggest I was only joking about love and partnership's
being important to me. Underlying their response was the
assumption that women who have chosen to devote a lot
of energy to work see this choice as more important than
love. They could not accept that a woman could be loving

and passionately committed to work. Unable to see the way these two passions enhance and reinforce each other, they wanted to negate my right to love.

Passionate devotion to work has always heightened my awareness of the importance of love. On the desk where I write sits a card with Rainer Maria Rilke's lines stressing the kinship between love and work. With wisdom he writes, "Like so much else, people have also misunderstood the place of love in life, they have made it into play and pleasure because they thought that play and pleasure was more blissful than work; but there is nothing happier than work, and love, just because it is the extreme happiness, can be nothing else but work." Significantly, when successful women claim our right to wholeness by privileging love and work in our lives, we challenge sexist thinking that would deny us love as punishment for choosing to value work. I place love before work because I know that without a sound foundation of self-love, I risk undermining my value and the value of all I accomplish through work.

Self-love can sustain us, but to thrive in community, which is how we live, we need to receive love from others. Contrary to popular opinion, powerful, achieving women desire love as much as we desire to be loving, because we know that love will enhance all areas of our lives, especially work. We desire loving partners to have the experience of heightened growth in the context of mutual sharing. Women in midlife know from experience that just as choosing the wrong partner undermines self-esteem, choosing a partner who loves us helps us maintain self-esteem when we are continually under attack. Gloria Steinem includes an afterword in the paperback addition to *Revolution from Within,* published a year after the hardcover. The afterword describes mass media's attempt to undermine the significance of this work by casting the writing of it as a sign of her "weakness." The vehemence of these attacks could have been undermining were it not for the overwhelming positive feedback received from readers.

When I began to write about love, every reporter that interviewed me wanted to know if I was "getting soft." These questions are not asked of men who write about love. No one wants to know if John Gray, John Welwood, John Bradshaw, or Thomas Moore is getting soft when he writes about love for these men have not been stereotyped as hard to begin with. Yet powerful women, especially intellectual women, have always been stereotyped as emotionally lacking. Our critical wit and wisdom are often seen as fueled by inner ruthlessness, by a lack of empathy for others, and not by keen insights honed by intellectual brilliance and deep, compassionate understanding of how our culture works. Readers could choose to interpret my writing about love as a testimony to my intellectual growth or to visionary insight, but sexist thinking devalues that experience and must make it appear that the choice to think critically about love is weak, aberrant behavior.

Vicious attacks and betrayal can assault the self-esteem of even the most powerful self-loving woman. And powerful women of all races and classes are always attacked. Self-loving, high-achieving women rely on the care of our loved ones to survive brutal attacks. We need feel no shame to speak of the importance of this love. I often remind friends and loved ones that every terrorist regime in the world uses isolation to break people's spirits. Undoubtedly, many women have turned away from the feminist project of female self-actualization for fear that they will be alone and unloved. The irony, of course, is that patriarchal devaluation of womanhood is far more likely to ensure that masses of women will remain alone and unloved.

Powerful, self-actualized women should feel no shame when we speak of our longing for a loving partner, our need to be supported by a circle of loved ones. It excites me to have reached midlife at peace with myself, pleased with my accomplishments, satisfied with my habits of being and my lifestyle. And while it does not diminish the joy in my life when I am without companionship, it enhances that joy when a loving partner is with me. All the women I know who have loving partnerships agree that these relationships support them in their continued efforts to resist patriarchal devaluation, to be all that they can be. Numerous feminist thinkers and activists, artists and writers, have been forced into isolation by an uncaring public that wants any woman who challenges the patriarchal norm to suffer. Living without communion, these women are often sick, lonely, bitter. They should never have surrendered their right to know love and to be fully self-actualized.

The fear of never knowing love keeps many females from striving to achieve all they are capable of. Letting that fear go would enable them to see that becoming all we can be gives us the foundation of self-love necessary for true fulfillment and draws love to us. Far too many women have allowed their choices to be informed by fear. They have refused to do the work of self-actualization, fearing it will keep them from getting a man, and even after making this sacrifice they find themselves alone. Usually this is a moment of awakening. Some women retreat into bitterness, but most work to recover the self they lost or never allowed to come into being. More often than not, these women give up on love, for they feel it was their longing for love that led them to needlessly sacrifice self. This is a pity. It was not love that led them astray, for without self-love they were not ready to know love.

Love is more present to women who know who they are, women who are fully self-actualized. This is the good news that self-loving, powerful women often keep to our-selves as though it were a treasure that will be lost if shared or for fear that we may seem to be bragging about "having it all." But the truth is, we can have it all but rarely do we have it all at the same time or in the order in which we want it. This absence of order is part of the magic and mystery of life. Rather than closing ourselves off from love, all women, especially those of us in midlife or approaching old age should sing love's praises. Love frees us to be ourselves and to be open to others' knowing us without shame or pretense. Dying without beloved partnership but surrounded by a circle of love, Elisabeth Kübler-Ross wanted to leave this message to the world, which she states in her autobiography, *The Wheel of Life:* "Everything is bearable when there is love. My wish is that you try to give more people more love. The only thing that lives forever is love." The female search for love is what life should be all about.

Love is the foundation on which we build the house of our dreams. It's a house with many rooms. Relationships are part of the house, but they are not everything and never could be. The key is balance. To live a balanced life, no group of women should feel they need to deny the importance of love. Self-loving, powerful, successful women know that true love abounds in our lives. Unless we tell the world our love stories, the myths that we do not want love and cannot get love will continue to act as warnings, keeping other females in check, keeping them away from the truth that genuine love will always lead us to be more fully who we are. Men and women who want to know love will find us, and we will find them.

Eleven

the search for men who love

LOOKING for love and looking for a man are two very different agendas. Most women without male partners are looking for a man. And guess what? Men are easy to find. Finding a man is not the same as finding love. To find love with a male partner, women have to be clear that this is our desire. The feminist movement exposed the harsh truth of woman hating. More than at any other time in the history of this nation, the word "misogynist" became commonplace. It was the shortcut way to describe a sexist, patriarchal, woman-hating man. But the other reality that feminism exposed, which was more uncomfortable for women to talk about, was female hatred of men.

Years ago, in the heyday of the contemporary feminist movement, I remember lesbian women joking all the time about how wrong the world was in casting them in the role of man haters, because everyone knew that if you gathered a bunch of women together in a room and started talking about men, the most vicious man-hating sentiments would be expressed by women who were with men and who were planning to stay with men for the rest of their lives. Hearing these comments again and again, knowing firsthand the truth in these words, I searched my soul to see what my honest feelings about men were. I determined that if I looked inside and saw that I really held men in contempt, I would cease considering them as potential partners and lovers.

When I looked inside, I found my thinking about men dominated by three images: my patriarchal father, whom I feared, at times hated, and wished was dead; my eccentric, antipatriarchal grandfather, whom I never feared, loved at all times, and wanted to live forever; and my playful older brother. My father did not care for our souls. He worked hard to care for our material needs. I appreciated this, but I never felt he loved me, even when I tried to please him, to meet the conditions he set. Even though I was told that he had been "mad about me," thrilled with his new baby girl when I was first born, taking me everywhere and showing me off, the dad I knew most intimately was cold, withholding, aloof, and emotionally shut down. Daddy Gus, my grandfather, was antimaterialistic and loved me unconditionally. Daddy was given to intense anger and now and then would throw a major violent fit. Our granddad was always kind and gentle, and he never spoke in anger. Our mother told us that he was not this way just with his grandchildren; he had been the same with his own children throughout their lives. She admired and loved him.

Then there was my brother, Kenneth. We looked like twins, even though he came first, eight months before me. Kenneth was everything a boy was not supposed to be: sweet, tender, playful, and fearful of being hurt. He charmed us with his humor. He was everything that Dad was not. His sisters loved him, and he loved us. We loved our brother, the eternal boy, ever Peter Pan, but we mostly feared grown men.

Honestly, had Mama's father, Daddy Gus, not been in my life, I believe I might easily have become a man-hating woman or at best a woman who just simply feared men. Lots of women fear men. And fear can lay the foundation for contempt and hatred. It can be a cover-up for re-pressed, killing rage. When girl children are learning what men are like within patriarchal culture and shaping our sense of them, we look to the male authority we know to teach us about masculinity. If the primary male figures in our lives are cruel, unkind, and in some cases violently abusive, this is the way we think men are. If the men in our lives—our fathers, uncles, grandfathers, brothers—stand idly by while elder women abuse us, then we lose respect for them. We do not forgive them their failure to protect us from harm.

I am grateful that the images of masculinity surrounding me as a child were varied. I knew that lots of men were "macho" like my dad, but I also knew there were men like my granddad—calm, gentle, and kind. These diverse images shaped my perspective. In my childhood there were men who were not ashamed to express their love of God openly and to shed ecstatic tears. These men were renegades, rebelling against the patriarchal norm. And they were the men I was destined to love, the sensitive, soulful, shy men who were looked down upon by the patriarchy. The men who inhabited my dreams were men of feeling.

When I entered wholeheartedly into feminist movement, I had the full encouragement of my male partner, whose personality, as it turned out, was a mixture of my dad and granddad. At that moment in our lives we had not fallen into the gender strife that would later lead us to separate. Then he supported my efforts to become a liberated woman. He was not homophobic. At no time did he worry about all the time I was spending with lesbian feminists, as some men did. In our groups women confessed that the men in their lives did not want them to hang out with lesbians. Their partners believed that they would turn into lesbians just by sitting next to one. We laughed at those stories. And we felt sad for these men who were missing out on friendships that might have changed their perspective on love and life.

In those days we used the phrase "male-identified" to describe women who did not necessarily like men, though they usually pretended to, but who supported any standpoint men in their lives held, who let their own opinions go to please men. Some of these women were subordinated against their will, but many of them were artful manipulators, pretending to embody the sexist feminine ideal even as they were contemptuous of real men, whom they believed to be stupid and childlike. Retrospectively, I can see that our phrase was incomplete. These females were not simply male-identified, they were patriarchally male-identified. Even then the most radical feminist woman knew that not all men wanted to be patriarchs. Male-identified women espoused the same negative sexist notions about gender common to any sexist man. They were not interested in the perspectives of progressive male advocates of feminism. To them, these men were not "real" men.

In our feminist consciousness-raising groups, women involved with men often had the harshest stories to tell. Knowing men intimately, up close and personal, they also knew the immediacy of male-inflicted pain. They knew about emotional abuse and domestic violence. Their rage at men was intense and unrelenting. At times it was infectious. It was difficult to hear a woman describing being raped repeatedly by an angry dad as a child, then running away from home with the first guy who was nice to her, only to find out later that when he was angry she was the punching bag for his rage—and on and on—and not feel antimale. These stories were commonplace.

Sitting in intimate circles listening to so much pain made us want to get rid of abusive men. It was easy to fantasize about finding them, interrogating them to discover whether they had ever abused a female, lining up the abusers, and blowing them away. Afterward you would go to the women they had hurt and assure them, "He will never hurt you again—never again." These fantasies did not emerge from an irrational urge to bash men. They were the stuff of feminist dreams of ending male violence against women. They were the stuff of wanting to know what the world would be like if it were a safe place—a place where women could roam freely, where we could "take back the night." Of course there were women in these groups who hated men and wanted revenge, but most of them expressed their rage and then went home to nurture and care for the men in their lives. Rarely were they lesbians.

Women's disappointment with men is rarely given a public hearing in our society. The flip side of the feminist consciousness-raising group was the informal gathering of wives in any community who played cards, shopped, and shared, in between the gossip about this and that, their rage and anger at men. Unlike feminists, they did not want men to stop being patriarchs; they just wanted men to be kinder, gentler patriarchs. Using feminist terms, we called these men "benevolent patriarchs." They were men who believed themselves to be superior to women and therefore felt they should rule over us. They just thought they should be kind providers and protectors. Prior to major feminist shifts in gender roles in our society, men who were cruel and abusive, usually found male-identified women to help justify and legitimize their actions. However, as feminist thinking about ending male violence against women, however diluted, has trickled down to the larger culture, most women will speak against male domination, against male violence, but still support patriarchal culture.

Women, like my mother, who have stayed in marriages with unkind husbands for more than fifty years, will condemn acts of cruelty and unkindness that as late as ten years ago they would have sought to justify or explain away. Whenever I would speak harshly about my father, my mother would always speak positively, reminding me of how steady a provider he had been. In recent years she has become more critical of his acts of unkindness. And she has grown bitter. Nowadays, past the age of sixty, when she makes comments about men in general, they are more likely to be negative than positive. As a mother of six grown daughters, several of whom suffered at the hands of unkind, abusive men, she, a traditionally male-identified woman, has begun to change her perspective. Now she knows that women are not to be blamed when men are treating us in violent and/or cruel ways.

More than ever before in our nation's history, women in general feel free to speak their resentment and rage at men. My youngest sister wears a button reading SO MANY MEN, SO MANY REASONS NOT TO SLEEP WITH ANY OF THEM. In the wake of contemporary feminist movement, it has become harder to articulate what we like, desire, and love about men. In this world where so many women work, few females talk about the pleasure of being economically supported by a male partner's income. And even a woman like Jane Fonda, married to one of the richest men in the world, who freed her from work, now testifies that she felt she was losing her identity in her marriage, and she left and began to create her own work projects.

Overall, women seem to agree that unless one has pleasurable and engaging pursuits, staying home is no fun. As should be the case, many working women find it wonderful to be home when they have a newborn babe. But even newborns grow up. The feminist movement created the social space for men to choose to stay home and be "househusbands," and like housewives they suffer the same complaints if they are unable to use their time away from a paid job meaningfully. In Arlie Hochschild's book *The Time Bind: When Work Becomes Home and Home*

Becomes Work, women acknowledged that they prefer working low-paying jobs even if they must do a second shift at home. They would rather work than be financially dependent on men. They would rather leave home and work even if they do not earn enough money to be free. If wages for housework had become a reality, this might not be the case. A domestic revolution might occur if wages for homemakers (like child support in some states) were automatically deducted from the working partner's paycheck.

Whether they think of themselves as feminists or not, more women than ever before face the reality that we live in a male-dominated society. And many women like it like that, as long as they derive benefits from men and no negative side effects. The negative side effects—tyranny in the household or sexual violence—no woman likes or wants. What most women do not choose to face is the reality that if you support patriarchy, you get negative side effects. As Elizabeth Wurtzel puts it, "It still feels like men have all the power. They still seem to obey their impulses to run away while women are enslaved to their impulses to run toward. As long as men continually get messages about avoiding commitment while women are taught to desperately seek it out, the sexes will always be at odds with each other and nothing will work." Of course, many men in patriarchal relationships deploy emotional abuse and physical violence to avoid intimacy. Perpetuating this violence makes the system of patriarchy work. Without male violence blocking the door, men might be emotionally open, they might find their way to love.

The popularity of books like John Gray's *Men Are from Mars, Women Are from Venus* indicates that lots of folks want to believe that women are innately different from men in personality and habits of being and that these differences naturally maintain the social order. They choose denial over facing the reality that the gender differences we were once taught are innate are really mostly learned, that while biology is significant and should not be discounted, it is not destiny. Nowadays almost everyone knows that not all men are stronger than women, or smarter, or less emotional, and so on. Sexist notions of gender rarely hold up when we look at real life. And they hold up even less when we go outside the boundaries of this culture and look at males and females in other cultures. Living in the United States, people easily forget or remain ignorant of the reality that women in other parts of the world often do much more physically arduous labor than do their male counterparts. Or that a great majority of men in the world are suffering from malnutrition or starving and are nowhere near the physical equals of females eating three meals a day who are citizens of rich nations.

The aspect of patriarchy that most women want to change is the unkindness and cruelty of men, their contempt and dislike of women. It is a testament to the learned ignorance of political reality that so many females cannot accept that patriarchy requires of men cruelty to women, that the will to do violence defines heterosexual, patriarchal masculinity. Liberal, benevolent, patriarchal writers, like John Gray, offer women strategies for coping with male and female mutual dislike. In all his work Gray basically encourages women and men to accept their differences and find ways to avoid conflict and abusive behavior. Superficially, it may appear that the popularity of his work exposes women's passive acceptance of patriarchal thinking, but it is in fact women's dissatisfaction with negative aspects of patriarchy that creates an audience for this work. While it may help women to cope with patriarchal men, Gray's work does not call for an end to male domination. Instead it perpetuates the conventional sexist belief that it is natural for males to desire dominion over others.

Many women feel despair about patriarchy's ending and try to find ways to cope with male domination that will heighten their well-being. It is certainly clear that sexist men are not rushing out to buy literature that will help them unlearn sexist thinking. Patriarchal thinking keeps women and men separate, locked in the artificial differences that Gray and other thinkers choose to regard as natural. Nothing was more frightening to women who wanted to be with men than a feminist movement exposing the depths of male contempt and disregard for the female sex. Luckily, by changing the workforce, the feminist movement did alter in fundamental ways how men see women. Yet despite the feminist call to change patriarchal thinking that denies men access to emotional growth, most men continue to believe it is "natural" for them to behave as though emotions do not matter, as though all emotional work, including loving, is primarily a female task.

The first chapter of Shere Hite's report *Women and Love* cites "men's emotional withholding and distancing," their "reluctance to talk about personal thoughts and feelings," as a major problem. Hite reports, "Ninety-eight percent of the women in this study say that they would like more verbal closeness with the men they love; they want the men in their lives to talk more about their own personal thoughts, feelings, plans, and questions, and to ask them about theirs." I read this and remembered the card by the cartoonist Nicole Hollander that has an image on the cover of a woman sitting in front of a female psychic who stares into her crystal ball. The woman is saying, "Why won't he talk about his feelings?" And when you open the card, the caption reads, "At 2 A.M. men all over the world will talk about their feelings and women all over the world will be sorry." I purchased this card years ago and held on to it.

It reminded me of the occasions in therapy with my longtime partner when he would say that I always encouraged him to talk about his feelings, but when he did, everything he shared upset me. This made him want to remain silent. What he shared usually exposed that he was not the person I thought he was—that his values, ethics, and beliefs were radically different from mine. Try having a conversation with almost any man about whether it is best to cease sexual intercourse if a woman is uncomfortable. Most men want to continue coitus irrespective of what women feel. And if women talked to men about this openly, they would know that men feel this way before they engage in sexual activity with them. Much of what men have to say would be a turnoff, so no wonder many male seducers learn to keep their thoughts to themselves, the better to manipulate and con their female admirers.

Women are afraid to hear patriarchal men speak their thoughts and feelings when what they reveal expresses a reality vastly different from how we imagined them to be. Not only does this speaking expose our differences, the ways we do not connect, it exposes the possibility that we may not be *able* to connect. This is the possibility that the card alludes to. Patriarchal men seem to know this better than women. Their silence helps maintain patriarchy. When they speak thoughts and feelings that reveal pathological narcissism or negate a concern for love, it becomes clearer to the women they are speaking to that these men will not provide desired companionship or meet their emotional needs. Women do not want to talk to men about love, because we do not want to hear that most men are simply not interested in the subject. An honest patriarchal antagonistic groups to sexually mate with one another. It's clear that women who accept antagonism between the sexes as the "natural order" are happier in their relationships with men than are women who want an end to conflict. Shere Hite's report suggests that the vast majority of women want to see conflict end. Whether they are willing to give voice to it or not, this means that they want to see patriarchy end. As long as we live in a patriarchal culture, strife between women and men will be the norm. To some extent, changes created by the feminist movement that did not alter the underlying structure have made it possible for women and men to give voice to their discontent. It appears as though feminist thinking and practice made the conflict worse, when in reality had they been embraced by everyone, they would have resolved many conflicts.

It's hard for women to face the fact that patriarchy pits females and males against one another. When any woman first meets a man, she quickly decides, either consciously or subconsciously, whether he constitutes a threat. As long as the predominant response women have to men is initially fear, concern for our safety, then we will not have a world where women can wholeheartedly like men. Lots of women feel they need men in their lives, but far too many of them feel uncertain about whether they like men, because they do not really know who men are and what they think. Or if they do, they may confess to loving men but not liking them.

When women talk about what they find likable in a man, they name traits like kindness, strength of character, and integrity. As Harriet Lerner points out in *Life Preservers* in the section titled "Mr. Right and Mr. Wrong," "While individual taste varies, we want a partner who is mature and intelligent, loyal and trustworthy, loving and attentive, sensitive and open, kind and nurturant, competent and responsible. I've yet to meet a woman who says, 'Well, to be honest, I'm hoping to find an irresponsible, distant, ill-tempered sort of guy who sulks a lot and won't pick up after himself.' " Yet, she says, "Many women put more careful judgment into selecting a new toaster oven than they put into evaluating a prospective partner." Perhaps women suspend careful judgment because deep down they know that to exercise it might mean doing without male partnership for long periods of time.

Looking for a man who can love is a search that can take ages. Most men are still clinging to the rewards and forms of power patriarchy extends to them for not being loving. Since patriarchy wounds men in the place where they could be self-loving by imposing on them an identity that denies their wholeness, in order to know love, men must challenge patriarchy. And there are men who are rising to the challenge. These are the men women want to find.

I was way past thirty before I made that useful list of qualities I most desired in a partner. At the top of my list of ten qualities were honesty and openness. Had I applied this standard of evaluation, I would not have chosen the three talented, attractive men who had been my serious partners before I made this list. They were, all three, liars. And I knew from the beginning that they were liars. I liked other traits and believed the lying would stop, which it always did for a time. When I faced this discrepancy between what I desired and what I had chosen, I was actually stunned. Therapeutic discussion of the thinking that was motivating my choices revealed a deep-seated message learned in childhood: "Men never tell women the truth." While I desired truthfulness from a male partner, subconsciously I did not believe that this was a realistic expectation. Clearly the message I had learned in childhood reveals stereotypically sexist thinking women hold about men. Women who truly believe that men can never be truthful can never feel as though they really know their male partners. If we do not know someone well, then how can we know we like them? And on what basis do we choose to love them?

When women eliminate sexist attitudes toward men from our consciousness, we are better situated to evaluate and like the real men we encounter. While I would not choose them as partners, I like some men I know who are sexist in their thinking, men who are liberal, benevolent, patriarchs, because I see other qualities in them I value. This does not mean I accept or condone their sexism. Knowing that both women and men are socialized to

accept patriarchal thinking should make it clear to everyone that men are not the problem. The problem is patriarchy.

Making the distinctions clear in *Fear of Fifty,* Erica Jong
declares, "The truth is I don't blame individual men for
this system. They carry it on mostly unknowingly. And
women carry it on unknowingly, too. But more and more I
wonder if it can ever be changed. . . . I believe the world is
full of men who are truly as perplexed and hurt by
women's anger as women are perplexed by sexism, who
only want to be loved and nurtured, who cannot understand how these desires have suddenly become so hard to
fulfill." Patriarchy can be challenged and changed. We
know this because many women and a few men have radically changed their lives. The men who are comrades in
struggle search for love to find the communion that is
needed to support their refusal to perpetuate patriarchal
thinking. The men who are our comrades in struggle show
us that they are willing to be challenged, that they are willing to change. As patriarchy changes, women are able to
love men more, and men are better able to love us.

Twelve

finding a man to love

WHEN I was a drama student in college, I was in a play about the war in Vietnam, called *VietRock*. It was a protest against war—against the state's willingness to send young men far from home to die. During the course of the play all the actors sang a song with these lyrics: "Don't put all your eggs in one basket. Baskets wear out and men die young. Better to marry trees and elephants—men die young." I entered college during the war years. The boys I knew and liked were on the road to becoming "new men." They did not want to kill anyone. And, moreover, they were certain they did not want to die.

The feminist movement was the best thing that ever happened to these boys, because it gave them the necessary tools to critique patriarchal masculinity. Unlike males before them who had refused to become soldiers, they did not have to be mired in lifelong, crippling guilt because they did not want to fight in wars. They did not have to pretend to be without fear. They did not have to act as if they loved violence. As the "new men," they were on the road to becoming lovers of life. Feminism gave them the theory to explain their resistance to sexist notions of masculinity. It gave them permission to publicly proclaim their love of life.

Writing these words more than thirty years later at a time when we are bombarded by successful "war" movies (*Deep Impact, Armageddon, Gladiator, Pearl Harbor*) that glamorize killing, I fear we are losing the memory of pain and loss our nation experienced when so many young men and women were sent away to die in Vietnam. The wars we see in today's movies are technological carnivals full of bright lights and intriguing ammo. Our boys do not lose these wars. They come home intact, full of glory. These movies—*Independence Day, Men in Black, Air Force One* (there are so many it's impossible to name them all)—though presented as entertainment, are also obviously prowar imperialist propaganda. They combine nostalgia and backlash. Nostalgia for the hyperglorification of patriarchal masculinity converges with a covert critique suggesting that men who do not want to fight in wars are not "real" men. These screen images are meant to wipe out the unglamorous history of boys and men dying young.

Just as the feminist movement affirmed the antiwar movement's stance on nonviolence, it set the stage for a full-blown critique of masculinity by calling for both the elimination of patriarchy and male domination. Most important, it called on males to reclaim their full humanity, to get in touch with their emotions, to speak their feelings, to let themselves love and be loved. Everyone forgets that the real force behind the feminist movement was individual women's disappointment with men. Even though equal pay for equal work and reproductive rights soon took center stage, the rage that had welled up began in male-female relationships. Women were tired of being treated like sex objects by the individual men they were relating to, whether as friends or lovers. From the movement's inception, visionary feminist women wholeheartedly believed that it would change the lives of men for the better. And it did.

While hard-core older patriarchal men and women held on to their sexism, large numbers of males struggled to rethink masculinity. Not surprisingly, men who were romantically involved with feminist women were the first converts. Threatened with the loss of meaningful relationships, they were willing, if not eager, to rethink old attitudes. It helped that the feminist movement and sexual liberation converged. Lots of men believed that there were goodies (not having to be sole providers, getting to have sex with liberated babes) to be gained by rethinking patriarchal masculinity or at least pretending to do so. While my lover, who was antiwar and pro–women's lib, supported my commitment to feminist politics and was himself a convert, he was never sure what the new masculinity should look like.

On one hand, while we both agreed on throwing out the old patriarchal model of male domination, we were not interested in what we jokingly called "wimp masculinity." These were the men who could not sustain an erection because to them all intercourse was rape. Or the men who subordinated themselves to any woman who raised her voice and turned up the heat. They were overcooked vegetables, and there was nothing desirable about that. Instead of changing the sexist notion that in every relationship there is a dominant partner and a submissive one, these men were taking the subordinate role. And while this was not desired, it was not clear what women really *did* want from "new men."

Men wanted to satisfy these new desires without giving up old habits and ways of being. Describing these confused expectations in *The Courage to Raise Good Men*, Olga Silverstein and Beth Rashbaum comment, "In response to the deep-seated cultural and economic changes of the last several decades, men are now expected to be all that they once were and more—sometimes in ways that contradict one another, that are downright mutually exclusive. The 'new men' are to continue to be strong, silent types while also being emotionally available. They are to be aggressive and empathetic, tough and gentle, hardheaded and sensitive, John Wayne and Alan Alda." In time these confusing expectations led many men simply to fall back into benevolent patriarchal behavior. By the mideighties, antifeminist backlash had pretty much silenced the voice of feminist masculinity, and there was no longer a public call for men to challenge and change patriarchy. Indeed, the tyranny of the hypermasculine reigned supreme expressed in popular culture by the increased dominance of misogynist rap. However, despite the backlash, nothing could change the fact that feminism had opened up new possibilities for male identity.

There was a "new man" in the making. This man was the offspring of women and men who had made their commitment, however confusing, to challenging and changing patriarchy. This man had eagerly taken women's-studies courses and had never embraced sexist thinking. Unlike the men we had known in the early and late seventies who were reluctant converts to feminist thinking, this new breed of male was born in a world changed by feminist activism; from day one he was socialized to accept equality of the sexes in every way. These males came into universities and chose to take women's-studies classes to learn more about how to divest of sexist thinking. They have been joined in this endeavor by older male peers. Their presence has been and is the real-life manifestation of the truth that feminist thinking is for everyone.

The propatriarchy folks controlling mass media created the image of feminists as antimale, but as more and more men became involved in the feminist movement, this false portrait could not be sustained. Men, changed by their own chosen involvement with the feminist movement, feel differently about feminism than men who were compelled to change their behavior to please the women in their lives. And younger men raised by progressive parents (many of whom are single moms) represent a new group of men who have not needed to divest of hard-core sexist thinking because it was never part of their consciousness. When I came to feminist consciousness in the late sixties and early seventies, we were debating whether women had the upper-arm strength to pilot planes. Now women pilots are the mothers of the young males who have no difficulty accepting women as equals.

The existence of new men who are antisexist in thought and behavior has intensified women's disappointment with patriarchal men. Now that some males have changed, all women have to confront the reality that sexist, masculinist behavior once believed to be innate not only is learned but also can be unlearned. These exceptional men offer to women they encounter in either friendships or romantic relationships the possibility of experiencing mutual love. The absence of a hierarchy in which someone is on top and someone on the bottom based on gender creates an environment where sharing and reciprocity is more the norm. Years ago I had intense conflicts with my partner over household chores, like who would do laundry, cook, or take out the garbage. He had to be convinced that he was not "losing his manhood" by doing his share. At times it was difficult. His male friends often berated him, telling him he was "pussy-whipped." Today I would not be attracted to a man who did not already assume responsibility for household chores. The good news is that there are men who embrace gender equality wholeheartedly.

When I began working on these chapters about men and discussed issues with women friends, whether they were partnered or not, the question often asked was "Are there any good men?" My response is "Of course there are." Since many of these women are in midlife, they often encounter men who are what I call "unreconstructed," who have not yet converted to feminist thinking in their private lives. These men may grudgingly or happily accept women as equals on the job but when they come home, they often want old sexist gender roles to be in place. While it diminishes all our lives that many men cling to outmoded sexism, it enriches our lives that there are exceptions, men who are as liberated as any feminist woman.

Many of these men are gay or bisexual. When they are straight, they are often under the age of thirty-five. I gave a talk recently and was asked during the question-and-answer period, "Is it true that you like younger men?" I answered with an emphatic no and stated that when it comes to choosing a partner, I am most attracted to men who are wholeheartedly committed to feminist thinking and practice. More often than not, the men who are the most committed to feminist thinking and practice are younger. Having spent more than a decade in a relationship struggling over gender issues, fighting about fairness, when I left that relationship I decided to choose men whom I did not need to convert to feminist thinking. The difficulty with conversion is simply that when a man changes to please a woman rather than from his own inner conviction, the changes are likely to be superficial. Most heterosexual women have been involved with a man who had some negative behavior they "fixed," only to find that in time of conflict or crisis that behavior resurfaced. Enlightened feminist heterosexual women in midlife, who have known both types of relationships— those in which we have to convince men of our rights and those in which men come to us embracing the truth of equality—know that once you have experienced the latter, there is little incentive to intimately engage unreconstructed men.

Males who have been raised from the time they were born to be holistic, to develop emotionally and intellectually, do not fear that loving makes them weak or that a powerful woman diminishes them. These men do not have to be fixed, because they are not wounded in the place where they would know love. In *The Courage to Raise Good Men,* Silverstein and Rashbaum amass convincing data to show that patriarchal masculinity prevents men from gaining the skills to be holistic, to have emotional well-being. They effectively challenge the notion that boys need to rebel against their mothers to achieve healthy separation, linking male violence and rage to our cultural failure to teach males emotional self-expression. Observing holistic men interact is the best testimony that their theories are accurate. Males who have been raised to be holistic, to be in touch with their feelings and able to communicate them, have more satisfying personal relationships than men who are emotionally closed and withholding. They are not ashamed to express their desire to love and be loved as boldly as any woman would.

New men see no need to dominate others in personal interaction. They can converse without making themselves the center of attention or their concerns the focal point. This trait pleases women. Most patriarchal men find it difficult to talk openly with women. And they usually dominate all conversations, even those with other men. They fail to listen to and are incapable of engaging in dialogue. In conversations they usually give speeches or tell stories.

All women, whether they see themselves as advocating feminism or not, like men who are able to listen and give feedback. Since talking is deemed feminine and silence masculine, men who talk openly are often regarded suspiciously. If heterosexual, they may be seen as gay by male peers. Yet most women long to know men with whom they can have meaningful, reciprocal conversations. This is a trait that makes the new man an alluring and exciting partner. Being in his presence is like being in the presence of a woman friend. In private conversations most women will admit that they are not impressed by patriarchal masculinity, that they would prefer the company of men who are as congenial and easy to communicate with as women friends. Women who say that they want male partners who are capable of mutual dialogue are often intimidated when they encounter men who honor female subjectivity. This may be especially the case in sexual interaction.

A few years ago I wrote a short essay for the collection *Transforming a Rape Culture*, describing my initial confusion and fear when I had a male lover who truly honored my body. Free to give full expression to sexual feelings, including the right to say no during any sexual interaction and at any stage, I was not sure how to behave. I was so accustomed to men who placed the satisfaction of their sexual desire over my and any woman's well-being. Unlike all other sexual encounters I had with men, there was never a moment when I had to pretend to feel something I did not feel. All my feelings were welcomed. Often in sexual encounters, women find that males respond with hostility if the woman expresses displeasure or discomfort. When I shared with women friends the nature of our interaction, they kept saying "Are you sure he isn't gay?" I learned an important lesson then. We demand that men change, and when they do, we are often not ready to affirm and embrace the liberation we claimed to desire.

New men can testify that the world is not yet ready for all they have to offer, because it is their behavior, more than any feminist theory, that challenges conventional accepted beliefs about the nature of masculinity. John Stoltenberg's *The End of Manhood: A Book for Men of Conscience* offers an honest account of the process men of conscience go through when they refuse to perform patriarchal masculinity. Stressing that such men learn to love justice more than patriarchal manhood, he writes, "Learning to live as a man of conscience means deciding that your loyalty to the people whom you love is *always* more important than whatever lingering loyalty you may sometimes feel to other men's judgment on your manhood." In the presence of liberated men, women's commitment to equality is tested. Individuals who see feminism as a way to place women on top are just as threatened by antisexist men as is anyone else. True equality means that females no longer have the luxury to indulge notions that we are the "superior sex" when it comes to matters of the heart, to caregiving, to acts of love.

Again and again I hear antisexist men talk about the flak they receive from women who want them to be "dominating but not too dominating." This desire is an expression of the confused expectations many women have who fear that the new man will not be masculine. Until our understanding of what it means to be masculine is changed from sexist norms, we have no standards by which to evaluate new men. When women are asked what trait they want to find in a man, they often say "strength." When asked to define what they mean, they usually acknowledge wanting males who are able to assume responsibility for their own actions, who can act decisively. These traits are ones many women seek to possess. They are traits present in mature, emotionally healthy individuals.

Embracing equality means that we all have to let go of our attachment to the idea of "gender difference." Affirming feminist masculinity may feel and look the same as feminist self-actualization in women. When I first began teaching women's-studies classes years ago, almost all my students were women. Slowly things began to change. Men who came to the feminist classroom expressed concern about gender roles. They wanted to find out how they could be self-actualized as males without conforming to patriarchal models. There is still not enough material to guide and direct males seeking feminist liberation. Often men who are antisexist go into hiding to remove themselves from the pressure to conform to sexist norms that are all around them. We need to hear their stories to know what liberated masculinity looks and feels like.

They are the "good men" women are looking to encounter. With them, no woman has to fear domination or the threat of sexual violence. They have no manhood that must be proven by aggression against womanhood. Offering a useful definition of the good man, Silverstein and Rashbaum share this insight: "The good man, like the good woman, will be empathic and strong, autonomous and connected, responsible to self, to family and friends, and to society, and capable of understanding how those responsibilities are, ultimately, inseparable." My work brings me in touch with many good men.

I believe that much antifeminist backlash began as a way to counter the movement of males, young and old, toward feminist thinking and practice. As antisexist "good men" make themselves known and let their voices be heard, women will turn away from men who are held captive in the prisons of patriarchal silence. Patriarchal culture was not disturbed when feminism appeared to be a woman-only thing. However, as more males became involved, feminist cultural revolution threatened to bring an end to patriarchy. To counter this hopeful and life-affirming change, feminist thinking was and continues to be viciously attacked. Yet no degree of antifeminist propaganda can change the reality that feminism has already created a world where there are new men who can offer women the mutual love we long for. Among these new men are loving gay folk who are role models straight men can learn from. When women who want to be with male partners search for love, we must first accept that we will never find it in the arms of patriarchy. When this acceptance is widespread, more men will choose liberation.

Traveling around our nation talking about love, I have encountered many men who want to be loving and who are willing to do the work. They find it difficult because there are just not enough support structures in place to affirm loving feminist masculinity. The path to male self-love is as arduous as the path to female self-love. We all usually have to begin this journey by going back to childhood to do the work of reparenting, to love ourselves rightly. I have heard the testimony of many adult men who were loving little boys. Their right to know love was mocked and ridiculed by adults. These men are working to recover the joy that they experienced when they felt they could open their hearts and just let the feelings come in.

Males who love are not yet as plentiful as the males who are yearning for love. The space of male yearning is the space of possibility. Women who love men and want them to be free willingly open our hearts to hear what men need to say as they search for ways to return to love. We are eager to read the books by men who are not from Mars but who are right here on this Earth giving and receiving love. They can offer us healing wisdom. When they let their hearts speak, the dialogue of love can commence and true heterosexual communion can emerge.

Thirteen

for women only: lesbian love

ALL women looking for love are not looking for men. Same-sex love has always been a reality; increasingly, it has become a choice. Today's lesbians are both born and made. By this I mean that the accepted belief that one's sexual preference has already been formed in childhood still holds true even as the reality of women's experience also stands as testimony to the fact that one can also choose to be a lesbian. And such a choice can be made late in life. Greater lesbian visibility in the nineties has led many women who had previously not considered women as potential partners to have a change of heart.

Significantly, when Shere Hite published her report on *Women and Love: A Cultural Revolution in Progress,* she included a section on women loving women. The data she reported that most surprised her readers stated that a large number of women who had lived most of their lives as heterosexuals were choosing relationships with women in midlife. Many of those women claimed to find in their bonds with females a level of intimate connection that they never had with men. Lindsy Van Gelder, coauthor of *The Girls Next Door: Into the Heart of Lesbian America,* openly "confesses" that she "was pretty happily heterosexual." While she enjoyed sex with men, she found that "the guys in my life were often emotionally disappointing." At the onset of the contemporary feminist movement, consciousness-raising groups were the place where lesbian women came and talked about their lives with straight women. It was there that many heterosexuals were first asked to explain why women disappointed with men did not look to women to satisfy their desires. Van Gelder recalls, "It was especially hard to envision all the qualities we loved in our female friendships—understanding, easiness, intimacy—in a hot sexual package." Married and monogamous, it took years before she allowed herself to experience same-sex love and finally to choose lesbianism— a choice that she wholeheartedly celebrates.

Like Van Gelder, I was nineteen when I first had confrontations with lesbian women about my choice to be with men. Unlike most of the women I encountered at feminist meetings, I was accustomed to being among women. Growing up with five sisters, I was constantly aware of female sexuality and the fear our culture has of female togetherness. Whenever we made friends at school and told them there were six of us, the other kids made scary sounds and acted as though our household was full of monsters. Adults were even more negative when they heard our household described—six girls, one brother, Mom, and Dad. Again and again as girls we heard folks express sympathy for our dad and brother that they had to live with all these females.

Long before I understood the nature of sexism, I understood from these reactions that females bonded together in groups were threatening. Underlying these insinuations about the danger of the female-dominated household was the assumption that one lone female is already enough of a "problem." Women, we learned in our church, were the carriers of evil. The more women gathered, the greater the possibility of sin and perversion, or so the sexist stereotypes warned us. But we knew from experience that females together could produce households of sharing and mutuality, of pleasure and delight, households where womanness was at the center and mattered. Maybe because there were so many of us girls it was simply assumed that, as at the all-girl school or women's college, there was bound to be a lesbian among us. Or as boys often suggested, maybe my sisters and I were all lesbians.

Raised in such an atmosphere, I always understood that lesbianism was a choice a woman could make. In our small town the women known to be lesbians were usually married. While some folks gossiped about their behavior and some folks shunned them, our mother talked about these women as if they were intriguing and fascinating. When I entered college and threw myself passionately into the feminist movement, I was not threatened when interrogated about my relationships with men. I was not afraid to be in groups of women. And the idea of women loving women made perfect sense to me. All around me there were young women who were scared of coming to those all-women groups. Some of them feared that just by association they might "become" lesbians. Now, almost thirty years later, I see that they were right in assuming that the more we strip away sexist thinking, the more we let go of heterosexism (that is, the belief that it is "natural" for women and men to mate with one another rather than a culturally learned practice), the more likely we are to see women as potential partners.

In their book *The Girls Next Door*, Lindsy Van Gelder and Pamela Brandt did not explore with any depth the reasons that lesbianism became more chic in the nineties, a choice any interesting liberated woman could consider, if not becoming a lesbian then at least having an affair with a woman. However, they gave as one reason "fallout from heterosexuals who, burned out on AIDS, date rape, sexual harassment, and the rest of it, were sniffing around for new takes on sex and romance." The other reason they offer sounds more plausible, which is that as more lesbians talked about the substantive nature of their love lives, more heterosexual women, especially those living alone in midlife, were seduced by images and stories of relational bliss. Van Gelder and Brandt understood this: "Lesbians often have a habit of falling in love with each other even when we're old, fat, 'unfeminine' or too smart for our own good. The lesbian social world is shaped by the fact that we're all women, the gender that's stereotyped, not altogether without basis, for nurturing, bonding, and wanting to talk endlessly about how we feel. Even when our personal lives are the pits, it isn't because one of us is from Mars and the other from Venus." *The Hite Report* called attention to the reality that more than 90 percent of straight women found emotional relationships with men disappointing because of male refusal to share thoughts and feelings. Women loving women surveyed in the report stated that they found their relationships satisfying because there was consistent mutual communication.

Any woman—gay, straight, or bisexual—living with, around, and/or among lesbians knows that there is as much conflict and strife in these bonds as there is in heterosexual relationships. In most cases it is the response to that strife that differs. And in other cases, especially those where lesbian roles mirror conventional sexist gender roles, conflict and strife may be responded to in ways that parallel rather than differ from heterosexual encounters.

Without romanticizing lesbian bonds in a glib or shallow way, we can acknowledge that women loving women for the first time in midlife often find these relationships more fulfilling than the bonds they previously shared with men.

Certainly among young women, especially the students I encounter, experimenting with relationships with both genders is almost the norm. An episode of the popular television show *Sex and the City* focused on the decision of Samantha, the oldest and most sexually confident and uninhibited of the four girls, to pursue a romantic affair with a beautiful female artist. Samantha shares with her friends the fact that she has already experienced same-sex intimacy in college. That this show is even on television is a measure of the extent to which there has been a cultural shift. Like the once-popular prime-time show *Ellen,* these shows challenge conventional sexist thinking about female sexual agency.

In *The Hite Report,* women testified that the desire to know love in the context of equality was the foundation that stimulated their interest in same-sex affairs and relationships. Importantly, women making new relational choices in midlife are more likely to have learned from experience what to avoid. By the time we reach midlife, lots of women are simply not interested in power struggles with either gender. *The Hite Report* included a section that posed the question "Are love relationships between women different?" One woman stated, "People in the women's movement said the problem with relationships is that men are so macho—i.e., they never apologize and they don't ask about feelings. . . . The best types of relationships are same-sex relationships, especially between women. They have the best chance in the world: they are more equal, and time together is much better quality. But even with all this going for them, there is no way that disputes won't come up. What you learn is to negotiate those disputes, and try to remain a team anyway. Women understand this better, the team concept." I know of no study done that looks at the differences between the expectations and relational satisfaction of women who choose lesbianism after years of being involved with men and women who have always lived as lesbians. It may very well be that women searching for love with women come to these relationships expecting to find greater sharing and emotional closeness and get what they are looking for in part because they are determined to create it and believe it is possible.

As a young feminist, fully embracing the idea that I could choose as a partner a woman or a man gave me a sense of personal power. I felt free from the heterosexist constraint to make love happen with a man. I no longer felt the sense of anxiety and panic about finding a partner that I had when I considered primarily men as potential partners. In conscious-raising groups we often talked about nonlesbian women choosing to widen the scope of our desire to include women as an act of resistance, one that would make us less vulnerable to being co-opted by men. Lesbian women among us supported this thinking because they were confident that if we chose to be women with women, we would be happier. Separatist lesbians were convinced that no real feminist could remain heterosexual, hence the popular slogan "Feminism is the theory and lesbianism the practice." The irony of this statement was that large numbers of lesbians were no more interested in feminism than were their heterosexual counterparts.

Writing by serious lesbian feminist thinkers usually disrupted utopian images of gay lifestyles. Answering the question of whether a "real feminist has to become a lesbian" in *Fugitive Information,* Kay Hagan knowingly responds, "Lesbians are not necessarily more feminist than heterosexual women; in fact they may not be feminists at all. As emphasized previously, no one escapes induction into the dominant-subordinate paradigm imposed by male supremacy. Lesbians, too, must work hard to create new ways of being in relationships. Avoiding men does not eliminate internalized oppression or unconscious obedience to oppressive values." Lesbians active in the feminist movement were more readily conscious of the fact that patriarchal men would not treat women well who challenged sexist norms, just as they were more aware that sisterhood would not mean an end to conflict between women.

Nonfeminist lesbians were much more inclined to

express the same pessimism about relationships expressed by heterosexual women. In May Sarton's journal of her sixty-sixth year, she responds to a young woman's queries about whether it is better to be with women than to be with men by cautioning her to remember that no matter the gender of one's partner, commitment to loving will determine the outcome of one's relationship. Sarton tells her, "I understand well that you are drawn to women especially at your age, it is so much easier in every way to have a woman lover than a man lover. And maybe it's not a bad way to come to understand about love . . . to come to love your body and appreciate all it can feel and give you and give someone else." Cautioning her not to close the door on relationships with men, she says, "I know you don't want to hear this but I must be honest with you. I want my influence not to narrow my young friends down, but to open the path for them." Wisely, Sarton stresses the value of commitment and tells her young reader, "If you truly love a woman then be with her and make a life with her. But a life of pure self-indulgence just won't work because it cannot feed your deep hungers. . . ." Clearly, women in search of love need to become mindful and aware of their true desires and longings. Many a lesbian woman has had her heart broken by a straight woman who was just looking for a new adventure.

Written in the early eighties, this advice seems especially prescient given how many young women today choose to have involvements with both men and women as they search for fulfilling relationships and try to understand the nature of their most authentic longings. While it may offend the sensibilities of "purist" lesbians who hate the idea of females' dabbling in "lesbian" relationships without making a commitment, young women's desire to explore a range of relationships is a resistance to heterosexism and patriarchal thinking and a challenge to homophobia. No matter the choice these young women make, in the end they are exercising a freedom to explore, learn, and choose that is a triumph of personal power.

The freedom young women have to choose female partners without shame has been given them by earlier struggles to end sexism and homophobia. Their decision to explore varied choices usually comes from their questioning of patriarchy and male domination and their desire to have different relationships from those that they have witnessed older generations having. Women loving women who choose paradigms of mutuality and reciprocity over domination and subordination are acting in resistance to everything they have learned about the nature of romance. Usually this will to resist has been forged in radical political movements for social justice or efforts to come to terms with unhappiness in other relationships.

Lesbians are no more socialized in the art of loving than is any other group of people in our society. Since the line separating a lesbian from a straight woman has been and remains a sexual divide, sexuality is often more discussed when same-sex relationships are the topic than are issues of love. When love is addressed, it is evident that lesbians, like their heterosexual and bisexual counterparts, are working to understand what women mean when we talk about loving. Relationships between women have been plagued with the wounds caused by disrespect and betrayal common to bondings in a culture of domination. Lesbians, like all women, come from families where dysfunctional behavior generated by domination, addiction, and the various abuses and violations they leave in their wake were the norm. The habits being learned in those circumstances have shaped adult behavior, including the practices of love. When one adds to these realities the effort to be self-loving in the face of homophobia, the struggle to love is as rigorous and intense for lesbian women as it is for anyone else raised in this culture, if not more so. June Jordan's essay "Where Is the Love" reminds us that "it is always the love that will carry action into positive new places" and that such love comes only when we have a secure foundation of self-love. Expressing her concern that we distinguish issues of sexuality from the practice of love, Jordan cautions, "I cannot be persuaded that one kind of sexuality, as against another, will necessarily provide for the greater happiness of the two people involved. I am not talking about sexuality. I am talking about love, about a steady-state deep caring and respect for every other human being, a love that can only derive from a secure and positive self-love." All women must work at the art of loving.

Key to that work is a commitment to honesty. Harriet Lerner's book *The Dance of Deception* is one of the few works that talks about the ways that learning femininity as pretense often alienates women from what we feel and know to be true. This learned behavior of pretense often keeps women from knowing their inner selves. Rather than moving inward, they struggle to please, becoming what others want them to be. Until all women recognize the damage done to self and others when we are addicted to pretense, we cannot progress on the path to love. Truth telling enables us to break through pretense and deception. Adrienne Rich suggests in *Women and Honor: Some Notes on Lying* that in honorable relationships couples have "the right to use the word 'love' only when we have made commitments to tell the truth urging us to remember: It is important to do this because it breaks down human self-delusion and isolation. It is important to do this because in so doing we do justice to our own complexity." Ultimately, she writes, "we can count on so few people to go that hard way with us." It is exciting that, more than ever before, women find women who are willing to embark on love's journey—who are willing to do the work of love. When this work is done, June Jordan proclaims, "we will know exactly where is the love: that it is here, between us, and growing stronger and growing stronger."

lasting love: romantic friendships

EEP, abiding friendships are the place where many women know lasting love. Women who are steadfastly heterosexual may live a lifetime without feeling true love between themselves and a heterosexual partner. The greatest tragedy of marriage within patriarchal culture is not that so many couples divorce but that an even greater number of couples stay together without feeling that they love one another. Over and over again as I talk with aging women who love about relationships, I hear us testify that the loneliness that may come with full self-love and self-actualization is far preferable to the loneliness of being in a relationship where love is not present. As a girl in Christian tradition I learned to ponder the proverb that cautions us to remember that "better is a dinner of herbs where love is than a stalled ox and hatred therewith." Loneliness chosen is always preferable to loneliness imposed.

In *All About Love: New Visions,* I emphasized that many of us learn to love not in the context of family or in romantic relationships but rather in the context of friendship. Sadly, sexist notions of romance that romanticize domination often keep women and men from learning how to love. Particularly, women and subordinated men often accept all manner of abuse in romantic partnerships, behavior they would find unacceptable in even the most casual of friendships. No wonder, then, that as independent women, especially single women, practicing the art of loving in midlife and beyond, we often cherish anew the friendships with both female and male friends that allow us to dwell in love, to know true love in relations with others even if we have not found such love in romantic partnerships.

In the Victorian age, romantic friendships existed for both same-sex friends as well as between a gay individual and a friend of the opposite sex. These romantic friendships lacked sexual engagement but were rich in erotic passion. Nonsexual erotic passion has little meaning in today's world. Nowadays the assumption is that something is wrong if an individual feels intense erotic connection with someone and does not allow that eros to lead him or her to sexual intercourse. Romantic friendships differ from other forms of friendship precisely because the parties involved acknowledge both that there is an erotic dimension to their passionate bond and that it acts as an energetic force, enhancing and deepening ties.

As women come to love in midlife, many of us recognize that we may long for deep and abiding intimate bonds of communion in love that are not sexual. And yet we want these bonds to be honored cherished commitments, to bind us as deeply as marriage vows. In keeping with the spirit of romantic friendships, individual women are choosing to create lifelong partnerships or to make life-long commitments with individuals they never live with, or live with for a time. Sometimes romantic friendships in which individuals live together are changed when one of the partners falls in love and makes a committed romantic union with someone else. But as it was in the nineteenth century, these bonds change but need not be broken.

When I left my first longtime common-law marriage, I knew that I would never again seek to find a loving part-nership solely with one person. I knew with my whole heart that it is best to have a circle of love, with committed bonds that extend beyone one privileged partnership. While my first partner was threatened by the deep roman-tic friendships I had, my next partner understood fully the importance of sustaining committed bonds of love in romantic friendships. Many abiding romantic friendships between women are broken when one of the individuals finds a mate or marries. This is especially the case when an individual woman does not have a feminist consciousness. Through feminist conversion many of us learned to place as much value on our bonds with women friends as we placed on partnerships with males, to value our nonsexual bonds with male friends as much as we value those in which we are sexual. That consciousness-raising must continually take place as long as patriarchy exists, for it teaches girls and women to value fully our bonds with one another, to value all deep bonds equally.

In a homophobic culture, deep, nonsexual, same-sex intimacy is often viewed suspiciously by straight and gay folks alike. For that reason it has been harder for females who share nonsexual, same-sex romantic friendships to talk openly about these bonds. When my romantic friendships (whether with an individual woman or man) become more visible to friends and acquaintances, they often want to suggest we are just repressing sexual longing. This is simply not the case. We are making a comfortable choice to use eros as a basis for strengthening a committed friendship. We may exchange vows of commitment that we deem as important to honor as those we exchange with romantic partners with whom we are sexual.

Often, an individual woman will establish profound bonds of love with a gay male. Sustaining, long-lasting, these commitments enhance the lives of both partners. In heterosexist, patriarchal culture, the only commitments that are deemed truly acceptable and worthy are those between straight women and men who marry. While the feminist and gay rights movements have changed this some, it is still difficult for nonsexual partnerships to receive the respect automatically given heterosexual relationships. A romantic friendship that lasts for a lifetime may be considered not as important as a sexualized romantic partnership that ends in a few years.

Romantic friendships are a threat to patriarchy and heterosexism because they fundamentally challenge the assumption that being sexual with someone is essential to all meaningful, lasting, intimate bonds. In reality, many people in marriages and longtime partnerships are not sexual; behind closed doors their relationships may be similar to, if not the same as, romantic friendships. Many single heterosexual women spend their time in relationships with men in which they feel unloved and unfulfilled, only to experience a moment of critical awakening in midlife, when they begin to do the work of self-love. And the outcome of that work is often the recognition that they would rather be alone than remain in unsatisfying partnerships. Or many of us are not able to meet men with whom we want to make committed partnerships. Finding a man to be with is a lot easier than finding a man who can be a loving partner.

In Barbara De Angelis's insightful self-help book *Are You the One for Me?* she lists traits we should look for in a partner. They are "commitment to personal growth, emotional openness, integrity, maturity and responsibility, high self-esteem, and a positive attitude toward life." In my conversations and interviews, it was rare for any female to admit that we had found even one or two of these qualities in male romantic partners. Most of us had found these qualities present in lifelong committed friendships, particularly romantic friendships. It cannot be stated strongly enough that patriarchal culture, and patriarchal domination of the psyches of men, encourage most men not to develop these traits. No wonder that heterosexual women who do possess these traits, who are ready to be in mature, healthy love relationships, usually feel they cannot find loving male partners.

This search for love often leads to great loneliness. Madonna Kolbenschlag in *Lost in the Land of Oz* states, "If the feminization of poverty is a reality of our times, so is the feminization of loneliness." This echoes the insights shared by Louise Bernikow in her book *Alone in America,* calling attention to the reality that women feel much lonelier than men in part because "the quality of relationships that satisfied most of the men I talked with left women hungry." Kolbenschlag comments, "a woman who came to me for counsel exploded in my office. She raged against fate . . . against everything that selected her to be born in this era. She grieved over the fact that so many women, like herself, were caught in a 'myth-warp,' doomed never to find a life companion because this generation is incapable of producing the evolutionary male that a woman's changed consciousness needs and expects." Our generation has produced progressive men, some of whom have learned to love and can be in healthy partnerships, but their numbers are small. Too many men, particularly those over the age of forty, are still trying to turn back time and remain in a state of arrested development. These are the men who do not have the traits De Angelis encourages women to look for in a potential partner.

Many progressive, liberated, loving women never imagined that we would one day turn away men as partners because we would see so clearly that they are not ready for healthy, mature relationships and may never be ready. Enlightened therapy and all manner of self-help literature has created an awareness of dysfunction in families and relationships. Not wanting to repeat past mistakes, many women have been religiously seeking guidance so that we can create lives rooted in peace, compassion, and love. To fulfill this longing, many of us have created a version of the "Boston marriage," making romantic friendships where we daily experience true love. Many consciously choose these relationships in midlife, when they recognize that they do not want the bonds heterosexual men are offering.

Certainly we hear more about the shortage of available men than we do about the huge numbers of men women turn away because these men are so emotionally shut down it is impossible to have a conversation with them, let alone a long-term relationship. Granted, most heterosexual women try again and again to entice men to do the work of self-healing and self-love so that the promise of true love can be fulfilled, but most men are just simply comfortable with the status quo, or they lack the courage to go through pain to the space of healing that would enable them to be mature, loving adults. Growth usually means that we have to experience suffering, and plenty of men want to avoid emotional pain at all costs.

In deep, abiding, romantic friendships, commitment to personal growth is a given. The work of healing is shared, the pain and the joy. More than before in our nation's history, young women better understand the obstacles they will face searching for love in heterosexual bonds. While they have not given up hope, they are more consciously aware of the need to create varied committed bonds. Recently *Ms.* magazine published an article by Pagan Kennedy, "So . . . Are You Two Together?" about two women in a committed friendship who are making a life together. Kennedy writes, "In the year and a half we've lived together, I have struggled with the namelessness of our situation. . . . Words offer shelter. They help love stay.

I wish for a word that two friends could live inside. . . ." Kennedy can learn from women who bonded for a lifetime in a committed friendship.

Though she toys with the phrase "platonic marriage" to describe the nature of her commitment, these new and progressive bonds are not based on the values most folks bring to marriage in patriarchal culture, and it seems to devalue their significance to apply this term. I like better the term one of the women she interviewed used, calling her relationships an "intentional" bonding. Describing this relationship, Kennedy writes, "The two high school friends, both straight women in their early thirties, moved to Boston together five years ago, knowing that they would share an apartment, and a life. . . . And yet, the two have left their futures open, and the promises they have made to each other are full of what-ifs." The what-ifs have to do with the possibility that one or both of them might marry.

Significantly, romantic friendships can coexist with the fact of partners' marrying, because their reason for being is not to replace marriage but to open up the possibility of sustained, committed true love existing among friends, and not just same-sex friends. No matter that our chosen relationship commitments change. Those of us who have long-term romantic friendships, some that have lasted longer than any of our marriages or partnerships, do not fear that these commitments will falter if we create other primary bonds. Our goal is to bond within a circle of love, of deep and abiding affections that are inclusive rather than exclusive. My male partner who wholeheartedly affirmed the primary bonds I had with individuals prior to my knowing him never tried to break those bonds or to join them. If he wanted to be with us sometimes, that was fine, but it was also fine if he had no interest in cultivating a close bond with my friend.

If younger women simply see romantic friendships as a substitute for the "real" relationships they hope to find along the way, these bonds will be fraught with emotional risk and the ongoing likelihood of betrayal. Most women in patriarchal culture have experienced the heartache of losing closeness with a female buddy when she finds her man. Since female allegiance to males upholds heterosexism, most men demand of their partners that they be the sole primary bond she holds dear. Ideally, when females and males have feminist consciousness that enables them to break with patriarchal thinking about romance and the notion that there should be a dominant party and a submissive party, then they can honor the bonds of love that they hold with one another and with anyone else.

Significantly, Pagan Kennedy states, "I've come to think of commitment as something beyond a marriage contract." She adds, "We're not sure what to call ourselves. We have no holidays. We don't know what our future holds. We have only love and the story we are making up together." Can we imagine that she would say of a committed relationship to the partner of her dreams "we have only love"? From the perspective of midlife, many women can testify that lasting love matters, whether we know it first or only in romantic friendships and/or in bonds of love with nonplatonic unions.

Lasting love is vital because we know ourselves differently in relationships of constancy where we have witnessed change through time. We cannot really risk emotionally in relationships where we do not feel safe. Commitment is the ground of our being that lets us make mistakes, be forgiven, and try again. Oddly, Pagan Kennedy initially seemed to imagine that she and her friend were creating a relationship whose path had not been charted. While she went back to and discovered the value of romantic friendship in nineteenth-century life, she did not report from the accounts women, who are not in midlife or aging, offer as evidence of the stability and sustaining tenderness of such bonds. She never uses the term "romantic friendship," which is the name that exists to define the bonds she describes. Folks may fear that term, because "romantic" in patriarchal cultural always evokes the possibility of sexual activity.

If women of all ages freely embrace the term "romantic friendship," we will open up the space where we can develop primary bonds in platonic relationships that are constant, committed, and able to last a lifetime. These relationships ensure that the woman who does not find a perfect mate will still know true and abiding love. And at the end of the day it is this love that sustains us and gives life meaning.

witness to love:

between generations

W OMEN who choose to love must be wise, daring, and courageous. All around us the culture of lovelessness mocks our quest for love. Wisdom is needed if we would restore love to its rightful place as a heroic journey, arduous, difficult—more vital to human survival and development on planet Earth than going off to slay mythical dragons, to ravage and conquer others with war or all other forms of violence that are like war. Wisdom is needed if we are to demand that our culture acknowledge the journey to love as a grand, magical, life-transforming, thrilling, risky adventure.

As wise, loving women, our gift to girls of all ages is sharing everything that we have learned on our path to love. I say "girls of all ages" because, just as pathological patriarchy has for generations encouraged men to remain emotionally crippled adolescents, there is a new breed of young women (the *Ally McBeal, Sex and the City* kind of females) who are also being encouraged to remain in a state of arrested development, to be emotionally underdeveloped, adolescent girls forever. The recent film version of *Charlie's Angels* provides a perfect cinematic portrayal of this syndrome. In the working world as the well-paid "servants" of the patriarchal man behind the scenes, Charlie, the angels conduct themselves as the equals of or superiors to men, whether in intellectual skills or in killing strategies (they murder as unemotionally, as brutally, and as swiftly as any macho man), but when it comes to romance, to *love,* they dither and titter and giggle like girls. They lose their minds, their perspectives. Behaving like underdeveloped adolescents is the sexual allure that ensures the angels will receive desired patriarchal adult male attention. These images send the message that to be an emotionally healthy adult woman is to be undesirable.

In our real lives, women who behave like emotionally underdeveloped girls (even if they are pretending) are often abandoned as they age by men who need the presence of a young and/or girlish female to feel powerful, potent, in control. Sadly, the harshest lesson learned by many females who spend their twenties and early thirties acting like adolescent girls to woo male attention and favor is that physically aging often leads the men in their lives to turn away no matter how girlie the women act and appear.

Wise older women who love offer to younger generations our lived experience gleaned from heartache, suffering, mistakes—all the plain old everyday experiences that helped us, yes, at times forced us, to become more aware of the pitfalls we need to beware, avoid, and eliminate if we are to love and be loved. When I witness the low self-esteem, the lack of self-love in brilliant young females in their late twenties and early thirties at the best institutions in our nation, females who have grown into womanhood at a time when women have the greatest degree of gender equality our nation has ever known, females who have had the benefit of feminist thought, movement, and achievement, it becomes all the more evident that there is a serious problem somewhere, a failure of thought and insight.

When I first saw the film version of *Charlie's Angels,* all I could think about was how glad I was to be in my forties and not receiving a cultural mandate telling me that I must be superwoman in the world, girlie-girl on the home front, and have the tight flesh of an Olympic athlete, while maintaining an ability to submissively throw myself at the feet of an all-powerful symbolic daddy named Charlie. The contradictions in this message are obvious. No wonder, then, that we have a nation of twenty- to thirty-something females addicted to antidepressants, angry at feminism, with cripplingly low self-esteem. No human could measure up to the standards mainstream culture sets for them. Life-threatening stress and depression are major factors in their lives as they struggle to be better than men on the job just to prove they are equals while grappling with the issue of emotional development and fear of being alone.

When I did lectures and workshops on my book *All About Love,* the only thing this group of powerful well-paid professional young women could say was "Who has the time for love?" And even more dire was their posing the question "Who needs love?" My generation of women learned the hard way that we could have all manner of success in our careers and still be undermined by crip-plingly low self-esteem. Now we know that the most femi-nist action any female can take on her behalf is doing the work of creating positive self-esteem, the foundation of self-love. For it is that grounding that prepares us to love fully and well. Whether we do the work of being an astro-naut, a lawyer, or a garbage collector, or whether we happily choose to be self-employed or a stay-at-home homemaker, wise women know that self-love will deter-mine the degree to which we will feel fulfilled by any of these tasks. This is why longtime feminist activist and ther-apist Phyllis Chesler writes in *Letters to a Young Feminist,* "In my time, older women told younger women very little about what it takes for a woman to become whole, stay whole, and survive. If they had, we'd have understood, awhile ago, that our first and greatest search should have been for ourselves, not for a prince (or princess), no matter how charming." Early on within the contemporary feminist movement, it was easier to blame patriarchy for all our female woes, rather than look within to see the ways in which we fail ourselves, the ways we self-sabotage.

Indeed, there is now a whole generation of individual women who came through feminism, who fought the good fight, who prevailed in all areas of their lives, who suddenly in midlife embraced anew old sexist ways of thinking about femininity. All around the world, females were shocked when activist Jane Fonda retreated into being a "subordinated rich man's wife." Most recently she has come to her senses and is now telling the world in popular fashion magazines how boring it was to give up on herself. Yet her betrayal of feminist thinking, of her own efforts to construct healthy self-esteem that is not based on whether you have a powerful Charlie-man in your life, has received far more attention than her confession that being a self-actualized woman in charge of her life is far more fulfilling than standing by your man, even if he is one of the richest men in the world. As Fonda put it, all this power just made him all the more "demanding" of her time, of her space. The relationship was engulfing. How can anyone be genuinely surprised by the outcome of this bonding, since it represents the traditional patriarchal model of marriage, the wife being absorbed in the identity of the husband?

Importantly, there are powerful twenty- and thirty-something new women who are in marriages in which they are the dominant parties. They may make more money than their partners and also make, unilaterally, the lion's share of decisions for the couple. These "bitch-goddess" girls often rule and have the power to assert dominion in ways that patriarchal husbands once did, setting the terms "my way or the highway." That they gain their power at the expense of male subordination is not a reflection of feminist success. It is a mark of the failure of feminist thinking to change the dominant patriarchal notion that in every relationship there is a dominant and a submissive party.

Sadly, I have found that heterosexual couples (and their role-playing gay counterparts) are often far more willing to reverse roles than to give up on the notion that there should be a hierarchy in which one person is the top and the other person is the bottom. In the aftermath of feminist change, it has become most evident that few couples are willing to do the work of love that would make mutual joy possible in partnerships. Since so many young women and men, as well as their elders, do not know how to love, it is easier to strike a bargain using the old norms of top and bottom, of dominant and submissive.

Mutuality, like love itself, must come through work. Wise women know that the happiest, most fulfilling committed partnerships (legalized via marriage or not) are those in which mutuality is the core value, in which the spiritual growth and development of each individual matters. Building the emotional space where mutuality can emerge takes time. Wise women who love know we have to leave time for love. Most folks will say that their loved ones matter most to them, but when you look at what they actually do with their time, it becomes evident that what they claim to love the most receives the least attention.

Women and men, girls and boys, must restructure how we spend our time if we want to be loving. We cannot be overachievers and perfectionist performers from kindergarten on in our public lives (the world of school and work) if we are to learn how to love, if we want to practice the art of loving. Genuine love requires time and commitment. And this is simply the case for love in the context of partnership. Self-love takes times and commitment, particularly on the part of those who are wounded in the space where we would know love in our childhoods. New women today, the late-twenties and thirty-something crew, are as reluctant as their patriarchal male counterparts to make time for love. Wise aging women know that one of the keenest regrets a large number of females experience in their lives is failure to understand early the power and meaning of love. Not only would that knowledge have afforded an understanding that would have prevented them from ending up emotionally abused and battered, it would have ushered true love into their lives sooner rather than later.

My hope for younger generations of women is that they will examine the unfulfilled spaces of their lives soon and boldly, unabashedly choosing to do the work of love, placing it above everything. Again and again it must be stated that when I talk about doing the work of love, I am not talking simply about partnership; I am talking about the work of self-love in conjunction with the work of relational love. Visionary feminist thinkers were among the first group of people to call attention to the disservice we women do to ourselves when we act as though it were important only to find the right partner, someone to love, rather than to choose a circle of love. When we place emphasis on building a beloved community, of which having a partner may be an essential part but not the whole, we free ourselves to lead joyous lives as single folks, and sometimes if not always as celibate folks.

Celibacy is often a liberating self-loving choice among women for whom the search for sexual pleasure has consistently led them down a self-sabotaging path. Writing about the reasons many contemporary heterosexual women choose celibacy in *The Coming of the Cosmic Christ*, Matthew Fox explains, "As women increasingly develop their awareness and consciousness and to the extent that

men resist doing the same, a sociological situation will prevail where many women will in fact not be able to find
men of their calibre and consciousness with whom to
share their lives. . . . Many women are finding celibacy a
better alternative than being victimized in abusive relationships." Joyless sexuality is not life-affirming. Within patriarchal intimacy, many women have sex against their will
and desire. Their partners may or may not be coercive.
Many men would be shocked to find that their female
partners are pretending sexual interest and feigning pleasure they do not feel and never feel.

The feminist movement many of us entered converged
with sexual liberation. And like many young women today,
we believed that it was important to prove our equality
with men in the world of casual and meaningless sexual
hedonism. Few of us feel that our lives or our sexualities
were in any way enhanced by these exploits. Often the fun
was not in the sex but in transgressing conventional sexist
taboos. It was not cool in those days, nor is it cool today, to
talk openly, about the desire to have sex within a loving
relationship. One of the most talked-about passages in *All
About Love* from the chapter on "Romance: Sweet Love"
was this one: "The best sex and the most satisfying sex are
not the same. I have had great sex with men who were intimate terrorists, men who seduce and attract by giving you
just what you feel your heart needs then gradually or
abruptly withholding it once they have gained your trust.

And I have been deeply sexually fulfilled in bonds with loving partners who have had less skill and know-how. . . .
Enlightened women want fulfilling erotic encounters as
much as men, but we ultimately prefer erotic satisfaction
within a context where there is loving, intimate connection." This is equally true for loving men. Therapist Fred
Newman puts it this way in *Let's Develop: A Self-Help
Guide to Continuous Personal Growth:* "the best kind of
sex, the sex in which there's the least amount of pretense—
the most gratifying and satisfying sex—is sex you do with
the person in your life with whom you are most open."
Not one woman in midlife that I interviewed for this book
saw sexual conquest or sexual satisfaction as the proving
ground for whether her life had meaning. All too often,
many of the women I interviewed who chose male sexual
partners felt dissatisfied with the types of sexual relationships they have had within patriarchal culture.

The most fulfilling, satisfying sex happens with the context of mutuality of consensual longing and desire. Andrea
Dworkin reminds us in *Intercourse:* "In fucking, one's
insides are on the line; and the fragile and unique intimacy
of going for broke makes communion possible, in human
reach—not transcendental and otherworldly, but an experience in flesh of love." Way too many young women are
still having sex they do not want in casual and committed
partnerships for fear of displeasing the men in their lives.
Wise women who love know that girls of all ages must

dare to take their erotic beings seriously. That means nurturing as early as they can in life a healthy relationship to their bodies, to sensuality and sexuality. The rise in sexual sadomasochism both in everyday life and in our intimate lives seems to be a direct response to the unresolved changes in the nature of gender roles, the fact that so much gender equality exists in the context of the same old oppressive patriarchy. Let's face the fact that it helps to eroticize domination if you feel you can't change it. Women and men do not know what to do, what roles to play. Sexual sadomasochism broadens the playing field, gives everyone access to more roles, without creating concrete changes in the ways power and affection are distributed in relationships, in our public and private lives.

Wise women who love have only just begun to create the maps of liberatory feminist sexuality, to chart a journey for women and men that will let us embrace sexual passion in ways that free rather than bind. We do know that women of all ages must continue our quest for sexual agency, that this is part of our assertion of healthy self-love. Knowing how to give love, we also recognize the love we want to receive. And that is a form of power. When females of all ages love our bodies and our beings, we are able to set appropriate boundaries, to make choices in which our well-being is enhanced as is the well-being of those with whom we choose to share sexual pleasure.

Self-actualization is no easy task. And it may well be

that there remains a body of women who find it easier to target men, to blame them for all that remains unfulfilled in their lives, than do the work of love. Wise women who love know that no matter the strength of patriarchy, women must assume accountability for changing our lives in ways that empower, for choosing to love, and for learning through love ways to overcome all the barriers that exist to keep us from being fully self-realized. Assuming responsibility for one's life, for one's happiness and well-being, is an integral aspect of self-esteem. Patriarchal men have often envied females the sexism that makes it acceptable for females to look to someone else to make us happy. This is the crucial myth wise women debunk for the young women coming along today, coming forward into midlife.

No one can bestow happiness or lasting joy upon us if we have not found the way to joy within ourselves. Self-knowledge is the way to find out what the secret of joy is in our individual lives. We may find our greatest joy in partnership, in community. Given the interdependent nature of our lives, of life on the planet, to share in communal encounter is vital for our survival. But the joy we share must come from within, must be rooted in our own soulfulness. It has been only recently in our cultural history that individual women have dared to speak openly about the importance of women's nurturing our souls, our spiritual selves. The bashing feminism gets in popular media keeps many folks from knowing that contemporary feminism served as a catalyst for spiritual awakening for many women, by telling them that the care of their souls mattered.

Celebrating a woman-centered spirituality that honors the Earth, the interconnectedness of all life on the planet in *Lost in the Land of Oz,* Madonna Kolbenschlag praises the female quest for union with the divine, for spirit-filled life: "Gradually I discovered through the medium of other women what I did not know and love in myself. My own experience and that of other women opened me to myself, to my reality as a woman, and to the Holy within me . . . I have learned in the company of whole and holy women to exorcise the unreal, to celebrate and ritualize the true and the real, to speak and have a new language, to feel the spirit through flesh and matter, to see everything—from within—as if creation were the Womb of God where, although we experience darkness and obscurity, there is also warmth, nourishment, movement, growth, connection, and delight." Wise women know that we must attend to our spiritual being. And there is no freedom to be found and relished when all is not well with our souls.

Learning to love has made it possible for us to care for souls and to rediscover the spiritual vision quests of female ancestors who offer us their guidance and wisdom. Every women should have, in her circle of love, companions of her soul. Soul nourishment sustains us when all the trappings of power, success, and material well-being lose meaning. To face life in all its fullness and complexity, what I like to call "the good, the bad, the ugly, and the obscene" without falling into corruption or despair, we need a soul that stands ready, to be our comfort and our shield. That soulfulness, that delight in facing and living life, comes to us as we journey on the path to love, as we search for love. It is the abundant gift.

True love is generous and ever replenishing. Wise women who love are not afraid to open our hearts to younger women so that they can speak to and with us about their deepest fears, needs, longings, and aspirations. Breaking down false boundaries created by sexist thinking that separates us, we lay the groundwork for true sisterhood to emerge, a solidarity through time and age that links generations of females together in strong ties of everlasting love.

(

Sixteen

blissed out: loving communion

FEELING that strong forces had caused women to become silent about our longing to love and be loved, especially women in midlife, I wanted to reclaim the discussion. Listening to so many women talking about finding mutual love for the first time in midlife, I thought it was time for us to share the good news. When I began writing, I was mainly imagining my audience to be women like myself, an over-forty crowd, one that had been around for the feminist critique of love and had come out on the other side of that critique.

Reading again Elizabeth Wurtzel's book *Bitch: In Praise of Difficult Women,* it saddened me whenever she spoke of love. Speaking of her peers (those under forty) she writes,

"None of us are getting better at love: we are getting more scared of it. We were not given good skills to begin with, and the choices we make have tended only to reinforce our sense that it is hopeless and useless." I cried reading this passage. It spoke to the loneliness and fear of not knowing love that I see in many of my loved ones, brilliant young women who stand on the threshold of promising and exciting careers and their male counterparts who have been my friends and lovers. I wrote my first book on love, *All About Love,* as a kind of source book, one that would both explain and guide. I teased a much younger ex-boyfriend with whom I have a primary bond that I was writing it for him so he could understand "what love has to do with it," so that he would understand "love is everything."

When I began writing this third book about love, focusing more specifically on women and love, I decided, in part after reading Wurtzel again, that it was important to speak not just to my age peers but to all women, especially younger women. My hope was that every insight I shared about the female search for love, about the value of love in our lives, would allay some of their fears and help make it possible for them to open their hearts, to love without fear. I am not happy to report that I began to understand love's meaning and power when I was in my late thirties. Even though I do not think I would have avoided suffering or heartbreak had I known better how to love then, I would not have wasted so much energy with lovelessness, suffered so much needless depression, all of which wore down my capacity to risk and trust.

That women who have suffered much heartache still long to love is a testament to love's power. It should give young women hope to know that so many of their female elders who had given up on love when we were younger now return to love to reclaim, rediscover, remake, and rejoice. We have learned how to distinguish real love from the fantasy of being rescued. Erica Jong describes this well in the autobiographical essay "Pathfinder," confessing, "Until my later forties, I honestly believed, in a gut way . . . that somewhere there was a man, better than the one I have, who had the power to transform my life. . . . That romantic dream of rescue is powerfully seductive to many women because it's so Oedipal—the fantasy of the all-powerful parents who will take care of you forever. The greatest freedom I have now is that I no longer believe that anyone else can save my life." As women truly love ourselves, a lesson many of us do not learn until midlife, though it should not be that way, we see how easy it is to save ourselves—to choose our own salvation.

One day the world will be utterly changed, and young females will find the path to love early in life; now it is still the case that many of us come to love through suffering that awakens us and demands that we take a deeper look at our life. This suffering, rarely chosen, is in its own way a preparation for passion. The root meaning of the word "passion" is "to suffer." Passions we choose are different from those inflicted upon us because we are naive, ignorant, or desperate. The passions we choose awaken and transform us. That includes sexual passion.

I wish there were time and pages enough to record all the stories of women coming to an erotic awakening that many thought would never happen in midlife. Often female midlife erotic awakening is dismissed, especially by a male-dominated medical establishment, as though it were simply hormones run amok. Women know that there is a lot more going on in our psyches preparing us to open our minds and hearts for the most intense erotic experiences of our lives in midlife.

Menopause is an exciting moment for many women because it brings to an end cycles of bleeding that disrupted sexual pleasure and bodily comfort. As all the over-the-counter PMS painkilling medication attests, menstrual cycles create all manner of physical discomforts that make being sexual a real drag for most women during this time. And even those women in longtime, pre-HIV, committed relationships who enjoy sex when they are bleeding admit that having to take care of soiled linen spoils the fun. I was always annoyed when my progressive, "feminist," male gynecologist tried to comfort me about the hysterectomy that fibroid tumors and constant bleeding were forcing me to have by telling me that I was going to experience a new lease on life. He told me sex was going to be great—like never before. I kept thinking, What did he know about it? Had he really surveyed women and asked them about posthysterectomy sex? At the time I could not find any articles that went right to the nitty-gritty and explained it all—how to have great sex posthysterectomy. Actually, I found more material cautioning that I might experience a lack of sexual drive. My doctor continually stated that there was no biological reason for such a change, that it was all mostly in the head and heart. If you think you will have great sex posthysterectomy or after any other major surgery that cuts away parts of your body, you probably will.

It took awhile, but he was right. I had no clue how much misery around my cycle had depressed and inhibited me sexually. Yet the pain and sadness I experienced posthysterectomy also depressed me. My reentry into heterosexual sex was scary. After your body has gone through what feels like an ordeal and is totally changed, it is not that simple to be sexual. Luckily, I reentered sex with a caring male partner sensitive to my needs and to what I had been going through physically. Swiftly, I renewed my passion for sexual pleasure and found it to be more intense than ever before. Some of that intensity was there because I no longer had the ups and downs that were common when I was bleeding.

Whether a woman's cycle ends because of unanticipated surgery or natural biological menopause, we believe that our sexual experiences improve in midlife and onward, first and foremost because we feel better about who we are. In Beth Benatovich's book *What We Know So Far: Wisdom Among Women,* a collection of interviews with women who are in midlife or beyond, all the women testify that it is greater self-knowledge that enhances their lives. They are clearer about who they are and what they want. And, most important, they are willing to take the risks necessary to bring new pleasure and joy into their lives. The writer Grace Paley testifies, "I always laugh when I hear people say they're fifty and they're finished. Maybe there's an expectation in America that past fifty, work will end, love will end, life will end, but in my experience, the opposite was true. Probably the most intense and surprising and exciting part of my life was in my late forties and fifties. You reach a point of some sense of what you can do in the world. You're freer than ever—free to do all kinds of work . . . and free to find each other, too. Among my friends, some of their best relationships were made after fifty." When I reached forty, I begin to listen with greater awareness and intensity to the wisdom of women in their fifties and older, because I felt they would give me the best and most realistic sense of the possibilities ahead. An overwhelming majority of women I interviewed and talked with believed that they were experiencing a new awakening. Even though we face new difficulties in midlife, the general sense was that we became more capable of coping with difficulty in a constructive, life-enhancing manner.

Women who were experiencing midlife and beyond as a time of loss and alienation tended to be individuals who had never been risk-takers and were unable to cope with a changed reality, with life not being as they expected it would be. An intelligent, attractive woman friend (though only in her mid-fifties) shared with me the fact that she no longer dates, no longer has sex. She mourned that men just didn't approach her like they used to. When I asked whether she approached them, her response was that she "just couldn't see doing that." She also could not imagine bonding with younger men. In her worldview a woman always chooses a slightly older man. This thinking keeps her stuck. Everything could be different if she changed her mind.

Importantly, there are women in midlife who choose to stop having romantic sexual encounters. To them this choice is life-affirming. One of the anonymous lesbian women interviewed for *The Hite Report* felt that after her mastectomy, her thinking about romance changed. She was no longer interested in coupling or embracing; instead she craved an erotica of being. While this disturbed her friends, who cannot imagine life without a relationship, she feels deeply content, saying, "Most of all, since the mastectomy, I realize more than ever that I love being alive. I love—I just love living. I like what I do. I like socializing. I love reading books. I love being alone. I love watching my VCR. I love going to parties. I love dancing. I love walking my dog. I love the beach. I get a lot of pleasure out of life. I just love the things I do." Her choice to cease coupling cleared the space for her to embrace a passionate existence. This may be what true love means in her life.

A woman's refusal to give up on love need not manifest itself in the conventional way of seeking a mate. It can manifest as seeking a more authentic relationship between self and world. In *Revolution from Within*, Gloria Steinem admits that for much of her romantic life she sought in male lovers forms of power she had not actualized in herself. Having made a conscious decision to let sexual romance go in her late fifties, she confesses, "I think the truth is that finding ourselves brings more excitement and well-being than anything romance has to offer, and somewhere we know that." This is especially true for women who have spent years, almost all their lives, subordinated to others or in self-sacrificial relationships to causes that may have left no time for the inner life. True love for them may be finding the soul mate within and nurturing that bond for the rest of their days. Everyone who interacts with them is given the pleasure of being touched by their new relationship to love. That is as exciting and stimulating as any romance. And as the recently married Steinem testifies, love can find you even when you are not searching for it.

Romance is different when two people approach each other from the space of knowledge rather than absolute mystery. No matter how well we get to know someone else, there is always a realm of mystery. Old ideas about romantic love taught females and males to believe that erotic tension depended on the absence of communication and understanding. This misinformation about the nature of love has helped to further the politics of domination, particularly male domination of women. Without knowing one another, we can never experience intimacy. But if males are taught from birth that the essence of their manhood lies in not allowing themselves to be known, it makes sense that there will be gender conflict, that it will appear that men live on another planet from women (that is, men are from Mars, women are from Venus). We would all do well to listen to therapist Olga Silverstein when she shares the crucial insight that "better communication skills" will not solve gender conflict until women and men accept that "it takes two whole people, who acknowledge that they live on the same planet—Earth—to communicate intimately." That is what women want. We want to know the men in our lives, whether they are fathers, uncles, brothers, lovers, friends, and to have this knowing be the basis for connection and intimacy.

Until women and men begin to think of knowledge as an erotic space of connection, both self-understanding and understanding of the other, we cannot change our sense of romance. Within patriarchal culture, most people learn romantic love as a union of opposites. Women have often looked to men, especially more powerful men, to fill the incomplete spaces in their lives. This never works. John Welwood introduces his book *Love and Awakening* by telling us, "We imagine that we should be able to establish a rich and satisfying relationship with someone we love, even if we have never learned to relate to ourselves in a rich, satisfying way. . . . We often don't see that how we relate to another inevitably follows from how we relate to ourselves, that our outer relationships are but an extension of our inner lives, that we can only be as open and present with another as we are with ourselves." In the past, females were not encouraged from childhood on to look deeply into ourselves and be utterly satisfied with what we found there. And it is still the case (as all the scholars of girlhood are reminding us) that the thoughtful, introspec tive girl is not as encouraged in her quest for selfhood as is her male counterpart. Women in midlife offer to younger women the truth of our experience; love comes only as we find love within. To risk self-knowledge is to begin love's journey.

Many women found, or find, love late in life because it took that long for us to awaken, to go back and do the original work of love—that is, the cultivation of care, knowledge, respect, and responsibility in relation to the self. When we do this work earlier in our lives, we have the skills that make loving and receiving love possible. Breaking with the misguided thinking about love that is common in patriarchal culture, we come to our search for love, to our relationships, knowing that there is nothing more romantic than the intensity of mutual connection. That intimacy lays the groundwork for two individuals to become soul mates—partners who are willing to do the work of love.

When we do this work well, true love becomes a reality. It transforms life. While no one can do the work of self-understanding and self-love for us, when we join together with another in committed love, we will be transformed. The self will grow and expand. This is why John Welwood believes that "true love always requires great daring." In midlife, women can find, and most often do find, the courage to open our hearts. This openness is the space where true love enters, intensifying our joy, heightening our awareness. Welwood offers this insight: "Awareness born of love is the only force that can bring healing and renewal. Out of our love for another person, we become more willing to let our old identities wither and fall away, and enter a dark night of the soul, so that we may stand naked once more in the presence of the great mystery that lies at the core of our being." Courage comes to us through experience.

It takes courage for women to challenge the seduction of domination, the making of love synonymous with erotic conflict between the powerful and powerless. A turning away from patriarchal perversions of love, the demand that we neglect the self to do for others, was certainly essential to women's collective growth. Yet we turned away from a negative vision of love without putting in its place a positive vision, one that would transform, that would heal and renew. In time, women began to feel shame that all the trappings of our newly gained equality and public presence did nothing to satisfy our souls. No wonder so many of us started going back to the old romantic vision of rescue and salvation in partnership, seeking an emotional safety that, though found, remains unsatisfying and unfulfilling. As we leave behind the stuff of the past that is mere burden, the relationships that bind rather than set us free, as we experience a change of heart, we develop the inner strength necessary to journey on the path to love, to make our search for love be a grand life adventure and a profound spiritual quest.

Along the way we do find soul mates, true friends, life companions. We find communion. Another great wisdom gift that women offer to those who have not yet discovered its pleasures is the wisdom that it is better to know the joy of dancing in a circle of love than to dance alone. While a romantic partner and/or soul mate may bring us joy, we add that joy to love already shared with all those who are truly primary in our lives—the circle of people to whom we turn, who turn to us—knowing that they will find us eternally there. No matter how sweet the love between two people, we ask too much if we demand that this relationship and this one other person be "everything." The truth we hold close is that "love is everything." And because love has this power, it is always there within us, within those we love. It offers to us the possibility of ongoing communion.

To commune, we come together and share our gifts. Illuminating this insight in *The Eros of Everyday Life,* Susan Griffin explains, "To exist in a state of communion is to be aware of the nature of existence. This is where ecology and social justice come together, with the knowledge that life is held in common. Whether we know it or not, we exist because we exchange, because we move the gift. And the knowledge of this is as crucial to the condition of the soul as its practice is to the body." It is only fitting that we, women having come so far in demanding recognition of our humanity, our equality, our gifts, and daily reaping the benefits of this struggle, wisely call for a return to love. Women in love offer to the world our inner gifts, seeking companions to share mutual regard and recognition—a communion of souls that will sustain and abide.